Forthcoming titles in the
JAZZ MASTERS series *will include:*

Dizzy Gillespie by Raymond Horricks

Charlie Parker by Brian Priestley

Gil Evans by Raymond Horricks

Phil Woods by Stan Britt

Lester Young by Dave Gelly

Duke Ellington by Peter Gammond

Oscar Peterson by Richard Palmer

Sidney Bechet by Charles Fox

Jack Teagarden by Sally Ann Worsfold

John Coltrane by Brian Priestley

Stan Kenton by Derek Jewell

Buddy Tate by Stan Britt

Gerry Mulligan by Raymond Horricks

Eric Dolphy by Raymond Horricks

Jelly Roll Morton by Peter Gammond

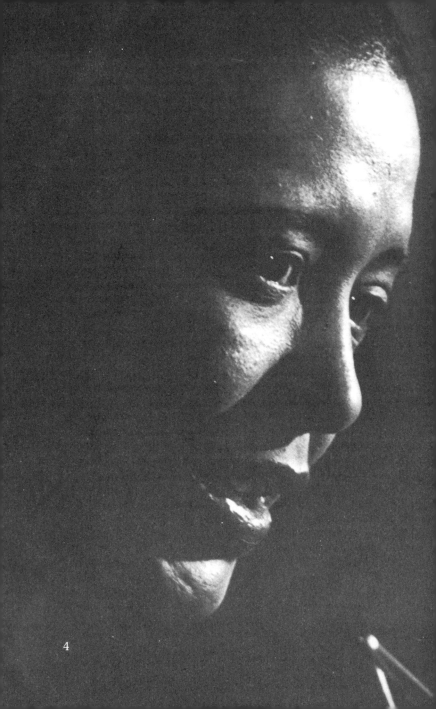

4

BILLIE HOLIDAY

Burnett James

Selected discography
by Tony Middleton

Spellmount
TUNBRIDGE WELLS

Hippocrene Books
NEW YORK

First published in UK in 1984 by
SPELLMOUNT LTD
12 Dene Way, Speldhurst
Tunbridge Wells, Kent TN3 ONX

ISBN 0-946771-05-7

British Library Cataloguing in Publication Data
Burnett, James
Billie Holiday.—(The Jazz masters)
1. Holiday, Billie   2. Singers—United
States—Biography
I. Title   II. Series
784.5   ML420.H58

First published in USA in 1984 by
HIPPOCRENE BOOKS INC
171 Madison Avenue
New York, NY 10016

ISBN 0 88254 907 3

Series editor: John Latimer Smith
Cover design: Peter Theodosiou / Tessa Mouqué

Printed & bound in Great Britain
by Anchor/Brendon Ltd, Tiptree, Essex

6

Contents

Acknowledgements / 7

Introductory: The Way It Was / 9

1   Baltimore Oriole / 16

2   The Lady and the President / 24

3   Fall Guy / 37

4   Fame but small fortune / 54

The Summing Up / 65

APPENDIX I: 'Lady sings the Blues' / 69

APPENDIX II: Discography / 71

Acknowledgements

Every writer on Billie Holiday must be deeply indebted to two books – her own autobiography, *Lady Sings the Blues* (Sphere Books) and John Chilton's detailed and devotedly researched critical biography, *Billie's Blues* (Quartet Books, 1973). There are also the critical writings of Leonard Feather, Nat Hentoff, and the late Ralph Gleason which throw valuable light on her life and her art. She has not been short of critical attention, but her own written view of herself, and Chilton's meticulous work, provide the basic ground from which all further examinations must begin.

Illustrations

Cover: Billie Holiday, mid 1950s (Courtesy Verve Records)

Title Page: Billie Holiday, mid 1950s

Ben Webster, Billie Holiday, Johnny Russell, with Ram Ramrizen (foreground), mid 1960's (Max Jones)

Billie Holiday, publicity still when she appeared with Artie Shaw's Orchestra, 1938 (Max Jones)

Billie Holiday, publicity shot, early 1940s (Max Jones)

Billie Holiday, from the film 'Sound of Jazz' (CBS)

Arriving in England, 8 February 1954 (Max Jones)

Max Jones, Louis McKay and Billie, after her Manchester concert, 12 February 1954 (Max Jones)

After the Albert Hall concert, London, February 1954 (Max Jones)

In her dressing room at the Chelsea Palace, 23 February 1959

Introductory: The Way It Was

When I was discovering jazz in the mid-1930s, I knew a dedicated and knowledgeable jazz enthusiast who insisted that there was only one trumpet player and only one band. Armstrong and Ellington of course. An exaggeration, no doubt, but as so often in such cases one with a hard kernel of truth. He did not mean to imply that there were no other good trumpet players or worthwhile jazz orchestras; simply that Armstrong and Ellington defined the boundaries and the priorities, each the ultimate in his particular field.

In the same way, it might be said that there are only two absolutely central, seminal and undisputed female jazz singers – Bessie Smith and Billie Holiday. Again, it does not mean that there are not and never have been others of importance and originality, only that these two defined the art of jazz singing, or more specifically jazz/blues singing, once and for all within their respective orbits. One might reasonably add a third dimension, that of gospel, and so include the great Mahalia Jackson as equal partner with Bessie and Billie, for it can be argued that jazz in the fullest sense has a threefold aspect – blues, gospel, and popular song. The singer and lyricist Jon Hendricks once said that 'it [jazz] all began in the house of the Lord'. Jazz began and initially flourished, along with ragtime and a number of other variants of American popular music, also in the brothels, dives, speakeasies and honky-tonks of the red light districts in the early years of the century. It also derived a number of its essentials from the work songs and field hollers of the slave era. It is easy to say that the middle aspect of jazz, that of the speakeasies, was instigated and encouraged by the era of Prohibition, that curious piece of legislation which turned the drinking of alcohol from an incidental nuisance into a social menace. But in fact it considerably predated the high years of the 1920s. As early as 1917 the U.S. Navy Department closed the Storyville 'red light' district of New Orleans because of its corrupting influence. If the denizens of Storyville actually did manage to corrupt the men of the U.S. Navy, they really must have known their business.

These early days of the origins of jazz and the 'classic blues' did not fall within the active lifetime of Billie Holiday. But they did all the same exert a considerable formative influence over her development as a singer. As a youngster she worshipped Bessie Smith, listened constantly to Bessie's records, and became hooked on her slow-drag tempo interpretation of the blues and popular songs of the day. In her beginnings, Billie Holiday longed to be another Bessie Smith. It did not work out that way; but it was Bessie Smith and Louis Armstrong who set Billie on her course. By her own admission these were the two primary influences on her career. From Bessie Smith she learnt the art of song. From Louis Armstrong she learnt how to use her voice as an expressive improvising instrument, which was to become one of her major contributions to the art of jazz singing.

Of course, Bessie Smith was not the only great blues singer of the classic period, and certainly not the first. There were great blues singers before her, and contemporary with her, prominent among them Gertrude 'Ma' Rainey, her own mentor and often referred to as the 'Mother of the Blues', as Bessie herself came to be known as the 'Empress of the Blues'. There were others too – Maimie Smith, Alberta Hunter (also known as Josephine Beatty and who continued singing into her eighties), Victoria Spivey, Ida Cox, Bertha 'Chippie' Hill, Clara Smith, Trixie Smith (there were a whole lot of Smiths around at the time, all unrelated). But Bessie Smith remains supreme. What Bessie did was to crystallise and define once and for all the essence of the classic blues form in the 1920s and at the same time move it closer to the idiom of instrumental jazz. As Louis Armstrong defined the essence of jazz improvisation of the trumpet, and Duke Ellington defined the true provenance of the jazz orchestra, so Bessie Smith did the same for jazz and blues singing in the musical and social context of the age in which she lived and worked. In her hands the blues moved out of the vaudeville tents and road shows and into the major theatres.

By 1933, when Billie Holliday made her first recordings with Benny Goodman, the era of classic blues had given way to the era of classic popular music in a wider sense. Indeed in the last years of her life Bessie Smith herself was adapting her style to the new concepts.

In the late twenties and early thirties there were a number of popular singers of some merit, a few of whom had a smattering of jazz feeling and recorded with some of the leading white jazz musicians of the time such as Joe Venuti and Eddie Lang, and the Dorsey brothers. Among these were Ruth Etting, Annette Hanshaw and Connie Boswell, but the two most distinctive and most jazz-oriented white singers of the 1930s (though by an odd coincidence both were of American Indian descent) were Mildred Bailey, who joined the Paul Whiteman organisation where she met and married vibraphonist Red Norvo, and Lee Wiley, one time wife of pianist Jess Stacy. Then there were the black singers and entertainers like Florence Mills and Ethel Waters, outside the jazz field but enormously respected by black audiences. There was also, more pertinently, Ivie Anderson, who sang with the Duke Ellington orchestra through the 1930s and into the 1940s until she was forced to retire because of the asthma which finally killed her a few years later. Ivie was the only singer of distinction Duke ever had on anything like a regular basis since, unlike Basie, singers were never Duke's strong suit. Ivie Anderson sang with style and elegance and an unmistakably individual tone; but she exerted little influence on other singers.

Thus Billie Holiday arrived on an already populated scene. Both Bessie Smith and Mahalia Jackson represented the culmination at a particular time of musical forms already formulated, but the art of the female singer of popular songs in the jazz idiom was still largely embryonic. And at the same time jazz itself, in its basic instrumental forms, was undergoing structural changes. Billie Holiday, therefore, can be seen to represent not the culmination of an already established art and style, but the beginnings of a new one.

Bessie Smith remains the key figure. Both Billie Holiday and Mahalia Jackson owed her an enormous debt, which both freely acknowledged. Mahalia Jackson always insisted that she would 'sing no sinful songs', while Bessie Smith sang virtually nothing else. Billie Holiday came somewhere in between: most of the songs she sang, and the way she sang them, came into a category that Mahalia would have damned as 'sinful'. On the other hand, there was often a curious quality of innocence about her singing.

One would hardly accuse Billie Holiday of being in any meaningful sense an innocent woman, yet her singing did quite often, and sometimes where one might least expect it, convey that quality or something very like it. It is part of what made her art so moving and so effective. It was also a large part of the hurt which life inflicted on her and which she inflicted on herself.

It is doubtful, however, whether she in her own mind would have been aware of the distinction, even have admitted it to exist in that form. Any suggestion that her songs were sinful or not sinful, sacred or profane, would no doubt have prompted from her one of her celebrated short, abrupt, unambiguous ripostes.

Set in the context of her times, Billie Holiday can be seen to have arrived on the jazz scene at precisely the moment when it was ready for her, and most urgently needed her. It is no coincidence that she and her greatest musical partner, tenor saxophonist Lester Young, came into jazz at roughly the same time and reached maturity side by side. They both came from the inside of jazz and in their respective and complementary ways gave a new twist to the development of jazz at the exact time when it needed to preserve and extend its vitality. Any art form, popular or academic, is liable to stagnate if from time to time its tail is not given a vigorous twist. Jazz in the 1930s had not so much stagnated as reached a point where it was likely to do so if not provoked into some fresh directions. Billie Holiday and Lester Young were among those who gave it an initial prod in the direction it had to go, along the road that was to lead less than a decade later to the so-called 'bop' revolution led by Charlie Parker, Dizzy Gillespie and Bud Powell, with the young Miles Davis and the iconoclastic Thelonious Monk in attendance.

Louis Armstrong, having moved the art of instrumental improvisation onto a decisively new course with the original Hot Five and Hot Seven recordings and consolidated it with the late Earl Hines in the second Hot Five series of 1928, then proceeded to do the same for jazz vocalism. Louis's 'scat' singing and manipulations of the lyrics and the melodic line, often taken for mere joking and fooling, or at best as a kind of freak effect, were in fact serious and successful attempts to use the voice as an improvising instrument. It became a common practice later, notably in the 'bop' era when young Sarah Vaughan used it with considerable success and Dizzy Gillespie deflated some of the surrounding pretentiousness with his use of it. And Billie Holiday was one who took serious note. She learnt from Louis how to use her voice instrumentally, and how to make it compete or collaborate on equal terms with the front line.

This had important consequences for her style and technique. Her claim that as a singer her two prime mentors Bessie Smith and Louis Armstrong is as easily confirmed by listening to her records as is the general view (her own as well) that Lester Young was her perfect musical partner. But no amount of 'influence' makes an original talent. All influence can do is to help direct the emergence of that talent. It is hardly too much to say that influence is nearly always pernicious. Billie Holiday herself influenced a large number of singers who followed her, mostly for the worse.

She wanted to develop the big voice of Bessie Smith, but such was not hers to command. And in the context in which she worked and the style of music she sang, it would in any case have been inappropriate. Her own voice, unique in tone and timbre, was neither large nor of the petite variety either. It lay somewhere between the massive tonal weight of Bessie Smith and the small pure tones of singers such as Mildred Bailey (known as the Rocking Chair Lady), Dardanelle, or ultimately Blossom Dearie, the epitome of the tiny voice in the intimate context. It was not the size or carrying power of Billie Holiday's voice that counted for most or determined the dimensions of her art. It was the way she used it, her unique ability to accentuate words and melody in such a way that both yielded maximum expressive force, often in hitherto unforeseen ways, and at her best, the sense of pitch that enabled her to explore harmonic and melodic implications with uncanny precision. Because she sang the popular songs of her day, many of them trite and banal before she came to them, she was frequently obliged to fashion gold out of base ore. Her art was a kind of alchemy. That she succeeded so often, against all odds and with material offering little apparent potential, is simply another and perhaps the final testament to her unrivalled art of communication. With most singers of popular songs, jazz or pseudo jazz, the result depends largely on what they can get out of their material. With Billie Holiday it was always what she put into it. That is why her failures tended to be so painful, so unnerving, so intolerable, as destructive as her most penetrating successes.

Despite her allegiance to Bessie Smith and the way she made certain of Bessie numbers, like *T'aint nobody's business if I do* her own, Billie Holiday was not and never pretended to be a blues singer. Her style was invariably blues inflicted, but she objected strongly to being classified as primarily a blues or torch singer. Bessie Smith had added a powerful jazz element to the pure classic blues style she inherited from Ma Rainey; Billie Holiday gave the screw a further turn and made popular song a vehicle for jazz interpretation and jazz improvisation. The distinction is fundamental.

Billie's great achievement was to turn frequently undistinguished popular songs into the materials of true jazz and the expression of genuine emotion; to inject into the common currency of the day a new depth and range. Even the best songs of the period, and it was after all a classic age of popular song, were further dignified and distinguished by Billie Holiday's treatment of them. She is not really a singer for adolescence or extreme youth, any more than Bessie Smith was. The very young can enjoy her as a jazz singer, on a level with the rest; but she was really one who yields her deepest secrets only when the listener has passed through some meaningful experiences of life and living. One of her characteristic songs, *Good Morning Heartache*, can best be described as *Bonjour Tristesse* grown up. She touched exposed nerves, largely because the life she led and her entanglements had exposed her own sensitive nerves. But more than that too; she was one who was born with an unusually exposed sensitivity. All her life she was congenitally incapable of skating over the surface of life or art, and in that respect she was a contradiction of and a reproach to the world of popular song from which she drew so much of her material.

The American critic Glenn Coulter once wrote: 'Next to Billie, others singing of love sound like little girls playing house.' And since the 'others' included Ella Fitzgerald, Sarah Vaughan and Anita O'Day, the judgment was significant, a

compliment worth having – if it were true.
   And it was true.

1

Baltimore Oriole

According to her own testimony, she was born in Baltimore on 7 April 1915 and named Eleanora. But the veracity of most of such information is suspect, as is that of many of the statements, her own and other people's, about the circumstances of her birth and early childhood. Indeed, even that famous opening of her autobiography, *Lady Sings the Blues*,

'Mom and Pop were just a couple of kids when they got married. He was eighteen, she was sixteen, and I was three.'

seems to have been more poetically than literally true. It made her mother, Sadie Fagan, thirteen at the time, as she herself later says, but that is something which does not tally with later dates and established facts. There are no available records, and poetic truth, not to say poetic licence, is deeply involved in Billie Holiday's life and must take precedence at many points in the story.

What is beyond doubt is that her father was Clarence Holiday, a guitarist who worked with several name bands of the period, most notably with Fletcher Henderson's. According to Billie, he went off to join McKinney's Cotton Pickers in the early 1920s. But that band did not become the Cotton Pickers until 1926, and no discography of that period in its history mentions his name. On the other hand, there is ample evidence that Clarence Holiday appeared with his guitar on many Fletcher Henderson recordings, and it was with Henderson that his principal career activity was undertaken. In his time he was a decided man about town with a sharp eye for the ladies, so much so that when Billie began to be famous he would ask her to be careful about calling him Pop in public since it tended to mar his image by hinting at more advanced years than he cared to acknowledge. But that was much later, after the Holiday family had broken up, which in fact occurred quite early on. Billie saw him from time to time, but her close relationship was always with her mother until the latter's death in 1945.

What ever may be the ultimate truth about the details, one

thing is certain: Billie Holiday was born in Baltimore. And there, seven years earlier, a little tubercular hunchback was born, William Webb, generally known as 'Chick'. During his short life Chick Webb became one of the most dynamic drummers of the 1920s and early 1930s and the leader of a band at Harlem's Savoy Ballroom which was the delight of dancers and listeners to good jazz. He died in 1936 at the age of thirty-two. The careers of Billie Holiday and Chick Webb did not cross at any significant point; all the same, there was a connection in the field of female jazz singers. It was with Chick Webb that Ella Fitzgerald first made her mark upon the jazz scene, and with that catchy but irritating little number *A-tisket A-tasket* achieved worldwide acclaim. After Chick's death Ella took over musical directorship of the band and kept it going for another couple of years. The connection is of some importance if only because Ella Fitzgerald came to represent the opposite pole to Billie Holiday in jazz singing.

Socially, Billie Holiday and Ella Fitzgerald shared one thing in common: they were both born poor and black. Thereafter, their paths diverged, and although each attained a unique place in their art, their paths did not coincide again. It was not only that Ella's life was never touched by the breath of public scandal, while Billie's came to many to represent little else. It was far more that their artistic paths drew ever more apart until there seemed virtually no common ground between them apart from broken marriages and social and emotional insecurity.

She did not have a happy childhood. She was frequently abused, ruthlessly exploited, and was almost certainly raped at a very early age. After the departure of Clarence Holiday her mother had to earn a living somehow. She went out to work as a maid and Billie was delivered into the care of a grandmother, in a household where she found neither kindness nor affection. Aside from rape, both actual and potential, she had the alarming experience of waking up one morning and finding her grandmother dead in her arms. It was enough to scare the wits out of any kid, and it certainly scared her. There was also a cousin who regularly beat her. One way and another, Billie Holiday's start in life was not auspicious.

Exactly when she started to earn by singing is also obscure.

She always sang about the place as a child and liked listening to records of her favourite singers, especially Bessie Smith. She seems to have heard her first jazz in whorehouses, something by no means unusual in those days. There was a bordello run by one Alice Dean, and Billie would run errands for her and generally make herself useful. Whether she actually engaged in prostitution at this time is likewise open to question. She was certainly arraigned for it on at least one occasion; but that does not signify much. The authorities then were in the habit of picking up anyone they had a mind to and making an example of whoever happened to cross their path. She lived her young life in a particular environment, emotional as well as physical, and it had some bearing on her subsequent career. One certain result was that for a long time she was 'scared to death of sex', and as so often, it led later on to a tendency to reactive indulgence.

According to her own account, her first professional singing job was at Jerry Preston's club, known as 'Pod's and Jerry's', or more formally 'The Patagonia', and after the end of Prohibition, "The Log Cabin". But she was certainly singing before that, and at times getting paid for it, if not on a regular basis. A number of people appear to have remembered her at work as something of a prodigy. She was emotionally as well as physically big even as a child, and it was partly this which got her into trouble with men and led to her being arrested and convicted for prostitution.

By the time she began her official career, she and her mother had moved to New York and set themselves up in Harlem. They had no money and by the time she went to Jerry Preston's joint on 133rd Street, she was pretty desperate. She began an audition, but not as a singer. She thought she might make it as a dancer. She did not, and could not, and never would. Still desperate and ready to do anything rather than find herself thrown back onto the streets, she said 'yes' when somebody asked her if she could sing. She had been singing all her young life and never thought of it as any kind of work, still less as a profession for which she might be paid. She sang, and it worked. She was hired, at eighteen dollars a week. That is how she remembered it, and there seems to be no solid reason to see it any other way.

It was at 'Pod's and Jerry's' that she first earned her nickname

'Lady'. In all such clubs in those days the girls, and there was always half a dozen or so working the tables, would collect the tips and pool what they got at the end of worktime. Some customers would give a girl something privately, not lay it on the table. Billie got on to this trick, and soon began taking all her tips that way and nothing off the tables. It seemed a fairly ripe way of carrying on, so the others started calling her 'Duchess', or just plain 'Lady', because they said she acted as though she thought she was a real lady. She had already taken the name Billie Holiday instead of Eleanora, because she was a fan of the contemporary actress Billie Dove.

It was at this club too that she had her first real love affair, with the resident pianist, Bobbie Henderson, a protegé of the great Willie 'The Lion' Smith who had been the previous encumbent. Billie was always somewhat coy about her relationship with Henderson, but it appears to have been widely known at the time, and for a while they were actually engaged. What she says about it was that this was the first time she had been treated like a woman, and that he, Bobby Henderson, helped quell the deep fears that still haunted her from her undermining past. It did not last, and by the end of 1934 it was over. However while it lasted it brought her some much needed reassurance.

It was around this time too that she was first heard by the impressario John Hammond. Hammond was immediately impressed and quickly arranged a recording session with a mixed pickup group under the leadership of Benny Goodman. Two comparatively cheap and chirpy numbers were cut – *Riffin' the Scotch* and *Your Mother's Son-in-Law* – but the record made no great impact and was in fact fairly ordinary. The real Billie Holiday had yet to stand up.

All the same, this was a kind of turning point. Not only did it inaugurate her association with John Hammond, who was to be responsible for organising the famous Teddy Wilson sessions a few years later, but she was also heard by Joe Glaser, one of the biggest and most influential agents and managers in the business. Glaser, who already represented Louis Armstrong and Mildred Bailey, immediately signed Billie and remained her agent for many years.

She was now launched on her career. She played most of the important clubs in Harlem and was soon appearing at the Apollo Theatre, the mecca in those days for stars of the entertainment business. She went down well at the Apollo and was booked for a second appearance, when she briefly changed her name to Haliday, ostensibly to avoid a clash of names with her father, but perhaps also a further indication of an inborn crisis of identity. She had already made a couple of appearances in films, one of them, *Rhapsody in Black*, with Duke Ellington's orchestra.

During most of this time Billie lived with her mother in a small apartment that became a meeting place for musicians and all sort of other folk, and almost a doss house for musicians down on their luck, who in those Depression days tended to be numerous. Sadie Holiday was a generous, warm-hearted woman of strong religious convictions who loved people and always did her best to help them, even if their gratitude was not invariably all it might have been. She always called her daughter by her proper Christian name of Eleanora, in public as well as in private, while other people usually referred to Sadie as 'Duchess', a name probably bestowed on her in the first place by Lester Young. Lester actually moved in as a semi-permanent lodger after finding a rat in the drawer of his hotel room and being terrified out of his sensitive wits.

Billie Holiday was never the easiest person to deal with. It was not that she was naturally cantankerous, simply that she would not be pushed around, forcibly objected to being exploited, and refused to compromise either for a quick advantage or to please anyone who was trying to put something over on her. She once said that you have to be black and poor to know how many times you can get knocked on the head just for trying to do something as simple as refusing to say anything unless you meant it. She had come to that conclusion as early as the age of thirteen, and it brought out a vein of obstinate honesty in her that bore upon all aspects of her life and career, perhaps not wisely but still unswervingly. She never gave up trying.

It came out when she was booked to appear at the Grand Terrace in Chicago. This looked like a big chance for her: the Grand Terrace was a prestigious club and the supporting band was Fletcher Henderson's (though Clarence Holiday was no longer a member of it). Everything went wrong. On her first night the manager, Ed Fox, got his knife into her. She sang her own way, the only way she knew and would ever sing, and the customers were not impressed. Fox panicked, started in on her, told her she sang 'too slow'. The upshot was a blazing row in Fox's office. Fox told her to get the hell out of his place. She responded by throwing the furniture at him, aimed an inkwell at his head which nearly decapitated him, and went, sacked after one appearance. Later, when she was famous and in general demand, Fox wanted her to go back to the Terrace. Billie told him straight down the line that she would never sing in his goddamn place, even if she never sang anywhere again.

After the Grand Terrace debacle, she and her mother found themselves stranded in Chicago with no money, no work and no prospects of any. So when they eventually made their way back to New York, Billie was in a black and potentially violent mood. She and Joe Glaser had never got on all that well, and the relationship was not made any better when instead of showing some sympathy with her predicament, Glaser sided with Fox's criticism and told her she must speed up the tempo and sing 'hot stuff'. Like all stupid and ignorant people, both Glaser and Fox seemed to think that 'hot' was synonymous with fast. But that was not Billie Holiday's way. Her approach was quite different. She herself knew that she was introducing a new style of jazz singing, and that it would take time for people to understand and appreciate what she was doing. She could, and sometimes did, sing fast, but her natural style was mid-paced with perfect timing, unique phrasing and extreme rhythmic subtlety. Ralph Cooper, who heard her in the early days at 'Pod's and Jerry's', was at a loss to describe her style; but he recognised its uniqueness. He told Count Basie that, 'you never heard singing so slow, so lazy, with such a drawl. It ain't the blues. I don't know what it is, but you got to hear her.'

That description of her singing as 'so slow, so lazy,' is illuminating. The particular way she sang, the relaxed delivery, the tendency to fall behind the beat and then ride over it, could be deceptive. It could make her sound as though she was actually singing slower than she really was. So when Joe Glaser started on about speeding up the tempo, Billie blew her top and told Glaser that he could sing any way he pleased, but she was going to sing her way or not at all. End of argument.

Another time she made a bad mistake through ignorance of what went on in the entertainment business. She was booked to audition for a show at the Nixon Theatre in Philadelphia, on a bill which also included Ethel Waters and Duke Ellington. She elected to sing *Under the Harlem Moon*, a popular number of the time, not knowing that it was Ethel Waters' speciality and a song in which she claimed proprietorial rights. The result was predictable: Miss Waters saw to it that Billie Holiday was summarily dismissed from the premises. It was a genuine mistake. Billie really did not know that the song was virtually Ethel Waters's property and that anyone else who was reckless enough to sing it in public was regarded as an upstart and a usurper, trying to cash in on Miss Waters's standing as one of the most revered black entertainers of the period. For once in her life Billie Holiday was obliged to retreat with her tail between her legs.

The next year, 1937, she suffered a severe blow. While she was fulfilling an engagement, she received a telephone call that her father had died, in Dallas, Texas. They had never been all that close, but they had kept contact, if only in a desultory way, and the news, coming unexpectedly as it did, was undermining. It seems that Clarence Holiday had been in poor health for some time, but because he was black and in Texas, he could not get proper help until it was too late. His lungs had been damaged in World War I, and in the end he was admitted into a veterans' hospital. Too late: he died of pneumonia and a haemorrhage. There had been a divorce some years previously. Sadie, good Catholic that she was, had never accepted it, but Clarence had married again and had several other amours along the way as well. At the funeral, Billie had to comfort her mother, deal with at least one 'stepmother', and perhaps two if certain claims were admitted, and some children. It was a harrowing experience; it saddened her at the time when her own life was by no means stable and clearly directed.

Though it is impossible to fill in with any accuracy the details of Billie's early life, there can be no doubt that the child was in many respects true mother of the woman. She never had it easy, and if she often made it more difficult for herself than it need have been, the fact remains that the cards seldom fell right for her. She did not draw well in the lottery of life, except of course for her marvellous talent. And that, if one is honest, does alter most of the perspectives.

2

The Lady and the President

He called her Lady Day and she named him The President. She was already known as Lady; now Lester Young took the last syllable of her name and added it to the other to make Lady Day. For her part, she thought Lester was the greatest, and since the greatest man around was the President (Franklin Roosevelt), she saw him that way and dubbed him The President, or Pres. Both names stuck. Lester Young had a highly individual way with words and language. He is given credit for having invented much of the 'hip' talk and words that became so fashionable in the jazz world of the 1940s and 1950s, including 'bread' for money, which he was apparently the first to use. He had an odd habit of calling everyone, male or female, 'lady' and would often refer to fellow musicians as 'those ladies'. It sometimes raised the question whether he was homosexual. He was not; it was just his way, the way of a fundamentally gentle, sensitive, courteous man who was constantly baffled and perplexed by the ragged world around him and did his best to avoid confrontations with it. So the appellation Lady Day was natural as well as apposite. For her, there was nobody above Lester, so he had to be The President, as was also natural and apposite.

They had a wonderful relationship, the Lady and the President, but it was a purely musical relationship. What emotional side there was to it derived entirely from the intimate artistic rapport. There was no romantic attachment, even though some have tried since to concoct one. All who knew them at the time were adamant that romance did not exist. Nor did either ever hint or claim anything to the contrary. They made · marvellous music together. They understood every musical and emotional nuance as they made it, but it never went farther than that. Perhaps precisely because it did not, the musical rapport was all the closer and more intimate, more subtle and interactive. Billie did have an emotional attachment within the Basie contingent; but it was not with Lester Young.

After her first recording session in 1933, it was to be another two years before Billie Holiday again entered a recording studio. Again it was John Hammond who was in charge of the proceedings, this time with a pickup group under the nominal leadership of Teddy Wilson, an elegant and sensitive pianist who had the right temperament for the job. Wilson was not a particularly assertive leader, and drummer Jo Jones recalled with some relish how they had to do some work on him before he got the right idea and fell in with the style of the predominantly Basie-based group gathered to partner Lady Day. But Wilson soon got the message and proved himself an ideal partner with enough 'name' to help sales. In fact, although the records sold reasonably well and did much to set Billie Holiday firmly before the discerning public, sales never did hit any highs.

The Wilson-Holiday sessions over the next two or three years, first under Wilson's name, later under Billie's own, drew upon whatever supporting musicians happened to be available at the time. Sometimes it would be members of the Basie band, sometimes Ellington's, and there were always independent men around who could be called on. That is why the personnels of these classics recordings tended to vary from date to date. It all depended on who chanced to be in town that day.

The best, though not the first, of the sessions were those that featured Billie Holiday and Lester Young in close partnership. Best of all, those that featured Buck Clayton on trumpet as well. If Billie Holiday and Lester Young formed the hard core, Buck Clayton made the third member of a memorable triumvirate.

The musical association of Billie Holiday and Lester Young raises a number of significant points in the contemporary evolution of jazz. It may be said that Billie Holiday was to Bessie Smith as Lester Young was to Coleman Hawkins. The coincidence, or more accurately the synchronism, was in a particular sense inevitable. The big voiced, elemental style of Bessie Smith evolved into the subtle, intimate art of Billie Holiday much as the big toned, rumbustious style that Coleman Hawkins had developed in the Fletcher Henderson orchestra during the 1920s evolved into the lean-toned, oblique, rhythmically and harmonically probing style of Lester Young. It had to be, not because one had to die for the other to live, but simply because no style can become definitive and final without first becoming stylised and ultimately degenerate. Both were inherent in the living body of the music called jazz. It is not too much to say that the style of Lester Young gave new life to that of Coleman Hawkins and the style of Billie Holiday gave a fresh impetus to the overall art of the female jazz singer. Though Bessie Smith died in 1937, by which time the classic blues style had more or less passed into history, she left a legacy and a foundation upon which much in the future, and especially the art of Billie Holiday, could be, and was, built. Coleman Hawkins lived on into the so-called modern period, the post-Parker jazz scene, but he was able to adjust his style and his musical thinking without, after a period of uncertainty, traducing his own powerfully individual style.

Duo partnerships in jazz have often been productive and memorable. One thinks particularly of Louis Armstrong and Earl Hines, of Joe Venuti and Eddie Lang, of the Parker-Gillespie link-up in the first days of 'bop', of the more recent cornet-guitar partnership of Ruby Braff and George Barnes. But none was more productive and more memorable than that of Billie Holiday and Lester Young. As far as the singer was concerned, the tenor-saxophonist was ideal. He was not the only one, but he was the best, the greatest, the President, the perfect partner. The way each responded to the other, the mutual prompting in the course of a piece, was frequently little short of uncanny. A sympathetic partner often adds a further dimension to the art of a singer, in whatever musical field. In this case it was uniquely so. What Joe Smith was to Bessie Smith and Tommy Ladnier was to Ma Rainey, so even more Lester Young was to Billie Holiday. It lasted only a few years, but while it did there was not another to match it. Fortunately, it is preserved for ever on records.

Exactly why the partnership broke up is not clear. They retained a deep regard for each other, and Lester seems to have been hurt that he was not thereafter asked to accompany Lady Day. They seem to have just drifted apart, and although they did get together later on, though not for recording, the great days ended with the Wilson-Holiday sessions under John Hammond's direction. Whatever the reason, Billie Holiday, when she needed a tenor-saxophonist in her later years, tended to call upon Ben Webster principally. Perhaps it was a matter simply of tone production. In the 1930s Billie's tone was hard and firm edged, and entirely suited by Lester Young's tone of the period. Lester's tone, early or late, never let you forget that the saxophone is a brass instrument played with a reed. It always had a metallic quality, in some contrast to the soft furry tone of Ben Webster. It could be that as Billie's tone lost its youthful cutting edge, and became in one sense more smudged, if still uniquely expressive, she felt that the more indulgent sound of Ben Webster was better suited to her. Perhaps after all it was simply that their 1930s partnership had drained their association of all it had to give, and that thereafter both Billie and Lester had to go their separate ways or fall back on the kind of repetition that could only have diminished the memory of the original achievements.

What is beyond dispute is that those 1930s recordings of Billie Holiday with Lester Young remain among the most perfect of all examples of distinguished popular music. Emotionally reticent, and because of that all the more probing, the Holiday-Young recordings have never been surpassed, and probably never will be. One after another the small masterpieces emerged. If one has to pick examples, *I Must Have That Man* will probably take precedence, but only as one among many. *This Year's Kisses, Mean To Me, Fooling Myself, Me, Myself and I, Travellin' All Alone, Born To Love, When a Woman Loves a Man*, one after another they came in the period 1937-38.

The first Wilson-Holiday sessions, however, did not feature Lester Young. Pres did not take part until 25 January 1937. Before that the sessions musicians were grouped around such men as Benny Goodman, Roy Eldridge, Bunny Berigan, Artie Shaw, Irving Fazola, and many others. When the Ellington band was in town and its men free between formal engagements, some of these were co-opted, Johnny Hodges, Cootie Williams, and Harry Carney. Indeed, the first Wilson-Holiday recording to come anywhere near taking off in sales terms was *I Cried For You*, made in June 1936, which had the theme statement by the incomparable Johnny Hodges, a musician who throughout his career was at home in any company and, whatever it might be, became an adornment to it. Here, as always, the Rabbit outlines a perfectly poised theme statement which forms an ideal prelude to Billie's vocal. It had not perhaps the emotional ambience of the later Lester Young creations, not because Hodges was a less talented or masterful musicians but simply because there was not the same personal empathy. In any case the song itself yields somewhat less in the way of emotional subtlety. In its own way this too is a perfect creation, a miniature masterpiece of popular song, Johnny Hodges the instrumental master, Billie Holiday the absolute mistress of the art of song.

Teddy Wilson used to tell how because of the dubious workings of the popular song business (or racket) controlled by Tin Pan Alley, they were seldom offered the top ranking hit songs that the system wanted plugged. Their kind of records were just not popular enough. This meant that they often had to make do with second line material. In one way, this could be seen as a kind of advantage. Anyone with a memory of those days will recall that the top selling popular songs were frequently of a banality and triviality difficult to believe. They were seldom if ever the class numbers from the pens of Rodgers and Hart, Cole Porter, George and Ira Gershwin, Jerome Kern, Harold Arlen (except on a off day), but the roughage of the trade that might momentarily catch the attention (or the inattention) of the general public. There were exceptions, but they were rare, and even then were seldom suitable as jazz material. The second line songs were often both better and better suited. Thus what was available to the Wilson-Holiday sessions tended on the whole to offer a wider and more usable selection. Billie Holiday had a marvellous ability to infuse a mediocre song with a distinction it did not deserve. But there were limits and some alchemies even she could not achieve. Fortunately she did not have to very often.

Once Lester Young had appeared on the sessions, the whole tone was subtly lifted. A perfect co-ordination became evident, appearing as if from nowhere, but in fact from within the evolving body of contemporary jazz itself. But it could also be dangerous. So perfect was the Holiday-Young partnership that any false note, however miniscule, in the rest of the accompanying group tended to stick out like a boil on the nose. It did not happen often, but sometimes it did. If Buck Clayton was the ideal third partner, Benny Goodman, who often sat in as a sideman and accepted (if reluctantly) a sideman's fee, often sounded way out of his depth, only his totally assured technique seeing him through. This was hardly Goodman's fault: his emotionally and technically spick and span style simply did not, and could not, accord with the penetrating subtleties of the Holiday-Young-Clayton interaction. John Hammond has suggested that Benny was aware of it and tended to feel uncomfortable in such disturbing company.

But for the most part, these Wilson-Holiday sessions with Lester Young produced music that if any recordings in the popular field can be legitimately be called classics must be accorded that distinction.

During the first half of 1937 Billie Holiday joined the Count Basie orchestra. There had been talk of it before, but she had heard loose talk of that description too often and took little notice at the time. Then the offer came, and she took it up.

The Basie band had hit New York from Kansas City at the end of 1936, and immediately made a huge impression. It was a band full of top class musicians and with a power and driving style that set the town by the ears. It was with Basie that Lester Young made his contact with New York, and so with Billie Holiday. For her it was a turning point in more ways than one. After all her troubles and disappointments, pinpointed by the debacle in Chicago at the Grand Terrace and the brush with Ethel Waters in Philadelphia, her star seemed suddenly to shoot upwards. Already established as a recording artist, she had still to make her name with the 'live' public. The Basie break looked like the way ahead.

The Count Basie band of the later 1930s rivalled the Ellington band in outstanding soloists and easily surpassed it in vocal talent. With men like Buck Clayton and Harry Edison (t), Dickie Wells and Bennie Morton (tb), Lester Young and Herschel Evans (ts) there was superb ensemble work. And the incomparable rhythm team of Freddie Greene (g), Walter Page (b) and Jo Jones (d), plus the Count himself with his own inimitable style at the piano, which always sounded (and still does) as though he is picking out a few notes with one hand while counting his money or flipping through the pages of *Playboy* magazine with the other. This was some band. Only Ellington at his very best could rival it. When Billie Holiday joined the band it already had the greatest of the big band blues shouters, Jimmy Rushing, on the payroll. The great difference between the Ellington band and Basie's (or anyone else's) was that the former was essentially a composer's band while all the others were and always have been arrangers' bands.

Billie Holiday's stay with Basie lasted less than a year. Exactly why she left has never been satisfactorily explained. She appears to have got on well with the other members, and musically she fitted in admirably. There was no doubt a little friction from time to time, inevitable in the circumstances of constant travelling and its consequent propinquity, and on the musical side there were moves, apparently supported by John Hammond in a way which undermined her relationship with him, to make her alter her style. She was urged to sing more blues and to modify the distinctive personal style she had by now completely evolved. To that she naturally objected, arguing logically that since the band already had a superior blues singer in Jimmy Rushing, there was no need for her to shift in that direction. She dug her toes in, on principle. She had already demonstrated with Ed Fox and Joe Glaser what was likely to happen if anyone tried to make her sing any way other than the way she wanted to sing. But nobody ever learns.

At this period of her life Billie Holiday was a cheerful, chubby girl, pretty and easy natured, and a good companion. Not yet had the statuesque woman of great individual beauty arrived. If emotionally she was already grown up, physically she still had a good deal of puppy fat. Nor had life cut so deep into her that there could be no going back. Her hard childhood and early youth had left a mark and a scar and she had already brushed with the racism that was to bedevil much of her later life and was in fact to hit her with full force only a year later. But the cheerful optimism of youth had not yet been squeezed out of her.

It was during this year with the Basie band that Billie had a romance with one of its members. It was not, as we have seen, with Lester Young, but with guitarist Freddy Greene. Later commentators have claimed that Freddy Greene was the one really good influence on her of all the many men to whom she was at one time or another attached. It never came to anything, sadly, because if it had, she might have been spared much subsequent sorrow and tribulation brought upon her by unscrupulous men who preyed on her and exploited her and did much to drive her towards the abyss and finally over it. She had already known Greene from the Teddy Wilson recording sessions, but the relationship was consolidated now when she was a member of the full band and going through the exhausting routines of continual travelling and interminable one-night stands. She herself said that during all that time she 'didn't see anything but the inside of a Blue Goose bus'. Under those difficult and demanding conditions, her good nature and cheerful disposition were much appreciated and helped to pass many wearisome hours. Much of the time was spent playing cards and money changed hands freely – all except Jimmy Rushing's. 'Mister Five-by-Five' kept his hands in his pockets and his money in his purse and would not willingly bale out those who had run themselves dry at cards or crap games.

Billie left the Basie band early in 1938, in some acrimony, after increasing disagreements with the band management. She was not sorry. Touring was not the way she liked or wanted to live and singing on a kind of routine circus round was not what she wanted either. She preferred the intimacy of clubs and the backing of a sympathetic small jazz group, or just a pianist.

However much she may have been disillusioned with touring, it was not enough to prevent her from doing it again as soon as she had left basie. She joined a new band which clarinettist Artie Shaw had just formed and was soon off on the road once more. Just why she stuck her neck out this way is another of the little mysteries that surround her life story. Partly, it seemed, it was a case of deliberate provocation, even of plain two-fingered bloodymindedness. Shaw muttered about needing something sensational to get his band off the ground, and Billie whipped back: 'Hire a Negro singer'. Shaw did just that. It was the spring of 1938, the place Boston and the venue for her first appearance with Shaw the Roseland Ballroom. It was not the first time a black singer had appeared with a white band, as she herself, and some who have taken her word for it, seem to have assumed, but it was still provocative. Shaw of course was perfectly aware of what he was doing, and to begin with at least indicated that he could and would deal with any repercussions. As a Jew he had himself run up against forms of race prejudice and held strong views on the subject. Billie too was willing to play her part, keep in the background unless actually singing, not push herself forward when away from the bandstand in hotels and restaurants where there might be trouble. But of course there was trouble, especially when the band went to play engagements in the South. Inevitably, the pressure built up. There were 'incidents', and although the band members supported Billie to the hilt, Shaw's own original determination began to falter.

It was not only the race question that complicated the issue. There were other factors. One of them, was Billie's style of singing, which did not always please the paying customers and was not commercial enough for the band management or the song pluggers. Shaw said later that it was during her stay with him that she finally recognised she would never be a big commercial success and that this was one reason why she turned to drugs to assuage her disappointment. It is not a wholly convincing argument, but it is worth noting. Certainly she ran up against prejudice against her style of singing as well as against her colour. How deep it really bit and how far it influenced her subsequent dependence must remain at best an open question. Shaw engaged another singer, Helen Forrest, to front the band, especially for radio shows, where the commercial pressures were most felt because of the power of sponsors. There are no records to show how she sang with the Artie Shaw band. She did cut one side, but it was never issued. From all contemporary accounts the contrast in style between Billie Holiday and the Artie Shaw band worked well. The members of the band were always delighted to have her with them. It was not their fault that things fell apart and Helen Forrest progressively took over the bulk of the singing.

Relations between Shaw himself and Billie Holiday remained good. There were inevitable raw edges when the going got rough, and Billie thought that at the end of their association Shaw was guilty of prevarication and timidity. But generally she admired him and thought well of him to the end of her life – and he thought well of her after some brief initial period of disaffection. There was even in the beginning a suggestion of something more serious between them. It was probably never all that serious, and inevitably it came to nothing. Later on Shaw gained a certain reputation and fame from the number of his marriages, but at this period in his career he had not yet acquired the habit.

The parting of Artie Shaw and Billie Holiday made the national headlines. Shaw always denied that race prejudice was the cause of the split. Certainly contractual difficulties with the record companies played a part. All the same, there were enough race problems to undermine any relationship. In many hotels and clubs she was not allowed to enter through the front door, use the main lifts, or even sit with the band. When not singing she was obliged to wait in some obscure upstairs room, and was generally treated with impertinence and at best with condescension. Ironically, the last straw came not in the South but in New York, where the band was booked for a residency at the Lincoln Hotel. The proprietress, Mrs Maria Kramer, tried to lay down the law about where Billie should sit, which door she could use, where she could drink (which meant that she was forbidden the hotel bar), plus other calculated insults. Shaw acquiesced, agreed to Mrs Kramer's demands, and that was the end. Billie had had enough.

Racism, however, was still not the whole story. Relations between Billie Holiday and Artie Shaw had in any case been in decline for some time. Part of it was due to the way she re-signed with Brunswick when he signed with Victor, making her inelligible to record for any other company, something which Shaw claimed she omitted to tell him. Then Shaw wanted her to sign a five-year contract with him, but she would not. There were also disagreements over money. So the Shaw-Holiday association ended, with some temporary rancour on both sides. It caused a disturbance and ruffled a good few feathers, especially in the Negro press which naturally put the whole thing down to race prejudice.

The ending of Billie Holiday's time with Artie Shaw was probably inevitable. The wonder is that she ever let herself in for it in the first place or stuck her neck out and laid herself open to all manner of troubles that were bound to follow. By a nerve-shattering piece of imbecility her colour actually cut back both ways on her. She was not particularly dark skinned; at times she could almost be taken for a southern Spanish woman. So while she was with Basie it was suggested that she ought to darken her face because some might think she was a white singer with a black band; but with Shaw she was once told to reverse the process and lighten her skin so as not to look like a black singer with a white band. It is hard to believe, but it is true. But then, as the jazz critic Ira Gitler remarked only a year or so back, 'In those days all America was racist. It still is.'

The engagement with Artie Shaw was the last time Billie Holiday ever worked regularly with a big band. In later years she occasionally appeared in concerts or made records with bands, including Basie's; but never again did she sing as a regular band member. In any case, she was never really happy doing it.

After leaving Shaw, Billie Holiday set out on the career as a solo artist which was to be hers for the rest of her life. In some ways, the break with Shaw actually served to advance her career – and once more it was John Hammond who set her off on her new course. The notoriety of her parting with Artie Shaw had made her name a lot more widely known, and because of it she was able to attract new audiences. It suited her to be out on her own. She had always known it deep inside herself. Her ambition to the end of her days was to have a little club of her own where she would sing only what she wanted to sing exactly the way she wanted to sing it; where no one could tell her what to do or go on at her for being 'too artistic'. She never realised that ambition, but as a solo act she was more free to do what she wanted, knowing that she was engaged to do precisely that, with no band management or song pluggers to breathe down her neck.

She never did make the top line with the general public or command the huge audiences she once hoped for, but once or twice she came near to it. The first time was in 1939, when she sang and recorded a number written specially for her and based on a poem by Lewis Allen. It was called *Strange Fruit* and it dealt with the lynching of Negroes in the South. *Strange Fruit* brought her another kind of notoriety and a more controversial reputation. There were and are those who believe that it brought her the kind of fame that did her artistic standing little good; others who have argued that the song did not really suit her, however much and however deeply she may have felt about the subject of it. Both points can be argued. What is beyond dispute is that *Strange Fruit* had profound implications for her, both personal and social. Whatever else may be said, her name became inseparably linked with it for the rest of her life and long afterwards. What is no less certain is that it is not a song she and Lester Young would have naturally cooperated on in the kind of perfection they once wrought together. The emotion is too raw, too far removed from the penetrating subtlety and almost eerie restraint of the work she once did so well with The President.

Although Billie Holiday and Lester Young remained good friends, their musical association was not altogether broken. In 1942 Billie went to California with a small band which included Lester and his younger brother Lee, a competent drummer, as co-leaders. They appeared at Billy Berg's Trouville Club in West Hollywood. The pianist in the band was Jimmy Rowles, who was to work with Billie Holiday many times in later years. It seems to have been a happy engagement: 'We used to rock that joint', Billie recalled, adding that many celebrities used to come in, including Bette Davis and Mel Tormé, and it was there that she first met Norman Granz.

Before that and after leaving Artie Shaw she had worked various places in New York and Chicago, including the Café Society and Kelly's Stables in New York and the Off Beat Room in Chicago. At Kelly's Stables she worked with a band led by Roy 'Little Jazz' Eldridge, one of the finest and most influential trumpet players between Louis Armstrong and Dizzy Gillespie. She was still making records, notably with Milt Gabler's Commodore label, in a series of sessions which contain some of her best work, with a supporting group led by trumpeter Frankie Newton, another fine and sensitive musician. The pianist here was Sonny White and at one time it was announced that he and Billie were to be married. But for various reasons, once again nothing came of it. Billie's emotional life was never all that stable, and became progressively less so as she grew older. How much the abortive affair with Sonny White upset her is hard to say. She was still unmarried, though she had had a number of liasons and was always strongly attracted to handsome men.

It came finally to a head in 1941, when she was working in New York at the Famous Door. She began going out seriously with one Jimmy Monroe, brother of Clark Monroe who ran the Uptown House where Billie had worked earlier and who had stood by her when she received the news of her father's death. She had known Jimmy then, but nothing developed until much later. Now she was going strong with Jimmy, and on 25 August 1941 they were married.

3

Fall Guy

It is not known for certain who first introduced Billie Holiday to heroin. She told Buck Clayton that it was an artist who lived in Hollywood. Or it may have been a young trumpet player named Joe Guy with whom she later formed a close and intimate relationship. They may even have been the same person. Whoever it was, Joe Guy or someone else, Billie never blamed him. She took her own rap, insisted that she was a big girl and knew exactly what she was doing.

What appears to have happened was the all too familiar story. She was introduced to heroin, found it made her feel good, probably at a time when she was in a low state, and when the reaction began to make her feel bad, upped the stakes until she found herself hooked and dependent. Like so many others, she thought she could handle it, found she could not, and subsequently had to go through all the trials and torments of addiction. She learned too late that it is a road down which many travel but none return intact and uncorrupted. It really is a road of no return and the only final release is death. She knew it soon enough, and she said it with courage and honesty, but could never kick the habit, despite help from friends and some authorities. In those days drug addiction in America was treated as a crime instead of as an illness. The treatment was crude and largely unproductive, and Billie was not the only one to find the attitude of the courts and the police, who constantly hounded her, tended to push her back into dependence. She had to learn the hardest of lessons that dope does not make you feel good, live good or sing better. It destroys and it gives nothing in return.

She had been an enthusiastic pot smoker since she was a girl. She took to reefers as a kid, and although it frightened the life out of her mother when she found out, it does not appear to have done her a lot of harm to begin with. But inevitably the question raises its cobra head: how much bearing did her early 'harmless' marijuana smoking have on her later nemesis, her tragic addiction to hard drugs? It is a question that has to be asked, even if there can be no definitive answer. The inarguable fact is that once she took to hard drugs, she was sunk and an addict for life. That it destroyed her in the end is not to be disputed, even thought there were other factors which contributed to that sad end and played significantly upon it. One of these was increasing alcoholism, in part resorted to as an attempt to counter the craving for heroin, but that too is revealing. It suggests an inherently addictive constitution, so that once she had started with either, the result was inevitable.

How much the deterioration of her voice in her later years was due to drug addiction is also a difficult question to answer. Certainly her general health and physical well-being were undermined, and since for a singer physical well-being is even more important than for an instrumentalist, in the sense that the actual tone production is dependent upon it in a specific way, such a deterioration inevitably had its direct artistic effect. On the other hand, through the later 1940s and early 1950s, when she was already heavily addicted, she could still sing magnificently, so that one is obliged to pause before setting her vocal decline entirely down to drug abuse.

As one reads through Billie Holiday's biography and autobiography and encounters the fact of the hard addiction and her possession by it, it is difficult not to clutch the head and cry out: 'For God's sake, girl, why did you do it?' She asked the question many times of herself, and could not come up with a convincing answer. And swift as gunshot the other question obtrudes: 'But if not, what then?' She always insisted that she only sang of what she knew and what she had experienced at first hand, and it had become recognised as one of her most distinctive qualities. The experience of heroin addiction must have played a major part in the making of her art. On the other hand, to find the real truth of the experience it is probably essential to go back behind the addiction to the complex personal reasons for it. It was these, rather than the experience of the addiction itself that constitutes the innermost 'knowledge' by which she lived and out of which she fashioned her unique art of song.

Insecurity lay near the heart of the matter, as so often in such cases. Insecurity of race, of family and social background, of artistic non-acceptance on the scale she longed and hoped for, of the necessity for reconcilliation of all these tangled subjective skeins. But most of all it was the insecurity in her personal life, most of all with her men. Though she had staunch friends and many cared deeply for her, she never had one relationship with a man which did not bring her deep hurt and enduring sadness. And in addition, more than one of them actively encouraged her drug habit. Though she was from time to time in her life, if not actively promiscuous then the next best thing to it, she longed for some lasting and deep rooted relationship of the kind she was destined never to find and which left her more than once stranded on the barren shores of loneliness and misery. When she was not being exploited materially and financially, she was invariably being exploited emotionally. No doubt she laid herself open, she was that kind of woman, but she suffered continual disappointment and disillusion. Her famous song *My Man* tells of much of her longing and inner anguish.

Her first husband, Jimmy Monroe, was feckless and given to smoking something more ominous than pot. When Billie and her mother smelt strange smells in the apartment, the lid blew and it was the beginning of the end. Billie herself was not hooked then. Indeed, some have thought that her realisation that her marriage was about to break down was one reason why she was open to the temptation of hard drugs. Jimmy Monroe also had a white girl in tow, and she was still around when he and Billie were married. One night he came home with lipstick on his collar. He started trying to explain, to make excuses. That got Billie's goat and led to another of her characteristic songs, her own *Don't Explain*.

It was soon after the breakup with Monroe that Billie joined forces with Joe Guy. It was also the time of her first steps on the heroin trail. It is certain that she and Guy made an awesome trio or haunted triangle with heroin the third party. She and Guy were never married, and seem never to have been formally engaged. For a few grizzly years they lived and worked and travelled together, and all the time Billie was sinking deeper into the mire of drug addiction. The upshot was inevitable. She and Joe Guy were arraigned on narcotic charges at two separate hearings, in Philadelphia in 1947.

A number of things had happened to her before that. She had taken a 'cold turkey' cure at a sanitorium, expensive but largely ineffectual. After it she went briefly to the New Jersey home of her current accompanist, pianist Bobby Tucker, where she received much help and kindness. However, she was soon back on the road again. Her stability and security were not helped by the death of her mother in 1945. Despite a quarrel a short time earlier, caused largely by Lady's disruptive life style and which resulted in yet another of her original songs, *God Bless the Child*, she and Sadie had remained close and helped each other when they could. Sadie was not fifty years old when she died. She had had a hard life but probably no harder than many others of her race and social position in those days. She had even achieved a mite of financial security by the time of her death. She worried constantly about her errant daughter, but her death deprived Billie of one more, and she might have thought the last refuge in a hostile world. Billie said after her death that wherever her mother had gone it could not be worse than what she had known down here. It was partly true, but not entirely. Indeed, Sadie actually went one better than her famous daughter. She achieved her ambition to run a proper restaurant of her own. It was nothing special and did not net a fortune, but at least it existed. Billie Holiday never did achieve her ambition of having her own club.

She was working all through this time, sometimes on a regular basis, sometimes as featured star or guest singer. And all the time she was deep into heroin. In her autobiography she puts great blame on the police and the federal agents who hounded her like a criminal, which according to the U.S. law of the time she was, often ensuring that any cures she undertook would be abortive. She tells how she shuddered inwardly when, on coming out of hospital, she saw federal vultures hovering and knew she was damned. It is an arguable point, but there is no doubt that it preyed upon her mind and did her harm. Whether she was totally sincere about wanting to be cured, there were certainly times when she genuinely did want it and tried to attain it. In such circumstances, encouragement is the only way to help, the smallest push in the opposite direction can be fatal.

On the other side were the pimps, pushers, parasites, sharks and every other form of lice who preyed on her. At her trial in Philadelphia the District Attorney said that she was charged huge sums for poor quality drugs costing only a few dollars on the market. She herself admitted that at one time she was spending as much as $500 a month getting the stuff. It was then that she said it was Joe Guy who put her onto it.

She was incredibly loyal to any man she cared for. It was actually her testimony that kept Joe Guy out of prison. She herself was sent down for a year and a day at the Federal Reformatory for Women at Alderson, West Virginia. She was subjected to another dose of 'cold turkey', even more brutal and ineffective than before. Famous she may have been, but she was not given any form of special treatment or granted other favours. She was treated like any other black delinquent, and that did not mean with kindness or consideration. She survived the experience and was released early, but it left its inevitable mark.

One result of her sentence and incarceration was that when she came out she was refused a working card by the New York police without which she could not work the city's clubs. There were other outlets and she was not without work, but once again the wrong pressures was applied in the wrong direction. She then fell into the hands of another unscrupulous man. John Levy manipulated an engagement for her at the Ebony Club, the police turning a blind eye. She soon fell in love with Levy, and it led her into more unhappiness. Levy took her over, body, soul and everything else. She could live in some luxury with Levy, but she had no freedom, no money of her own, and no independence. It was all very well, but a woman like Billie Holiday was not going to be taken over by anybody for long, on any terms. Whatever Levy gave, the motives were entirely ulterior, and of course it ended badly.

Maybe it was her own fault. Her choice of men was both naïve and obstinate. She was invariably attracted to bad types, and the good ones she knew and who cared for her, like Freddy Greene, Buck Clayton and Lester Young, plus several members of the Artie Shaw orchestra with whom she had worked, and a number of non-musicians, she never became really close to on personal rather than purely musical terms. A varying bunch of hoods, pushers, petty con-men and sundry leeches latched onto her for gain and sometimes pretended that they cared for her. But in her personal relationships and choice of men, she made wrong move after wrong move. She said herself, when she married Jimmy Monroe, that she was not the first chick to get married in order to prove something to somebody. When her mother and Joe Glaser warned her that she was heading for trouble and hurt, the reaction was predictable; she dug her toes in and went ahead. It was much the same with Joe Guy and John Levy: both cases of wilful obstinacy and a lack of judgment awesome to look back on.

Perhaps this failure in the emotional relationships was the deepdown reasons for her famous alliances with her dogs. She would not have been the first or last woman to bestow on an animal the love she could not find on the human plane. There was that 'skinny run-down mutt' that a West Indian friend had given her to take care of. She could not do that while she was travelling, so she gave it on to her mother to look after for her. They called it Rajah Ravoy (after a magician who was working around at the time when Billie herself was engaged at the Café Society). He was a great comfort to Sadie, and when he died she said she would not be far behind; and she wasn't.

Billie herself had two dogs which at various times shared her fame, and sometimes her notoriety. The first was the boxer called 'Mister' who was with her through good times and bad, especially the latter. 'Mister' was waiting for her when she came out of Alderson. She thought he would have forgotten her, but she was wrong. He nearly knocked her down at first sight. He was also with her on a subsequent night when there was trouble and another narcotics rap, and her car was peppered with police bullets. 'Mister' cowered on the back seat considerably nonplussed. Then she went to the other extreme, with her little chihuahua, 'Pepi', her constant, and towards the end her only companion. 'Pepi' actually accompanied her to jail on one occasion when she was busted, and survived her mistress, being looked after following Billie's death by her great friend and final confidant, a geologist known as Alice.

Billie Holiday certainly drank to excess, in addition to being hooked on dope; and it too contributed to the deterioration of her health and her early death. Whether or not she also had lesbian tendencies and practised them from time to time is another matter. The suggestion has been made, but there has never been any evidence to support it and all who knew her intimately, male and female, denied it hotly. She was an avid liver, and one able to resist all manner of temptations in respect of her art but virtually none in her private life. One reads the story of her life with a mixture of incredulity and horror. The question returns: Why did she do it – the drugs, the drink, the obviously destructive relationships? And again no answer comes back, except that she was that sort of woman, a terribly fallible, vulnerable and much traduced human being. And the second part of the question returns too: if she had not done it, not been that kind of human being, would she have been the marvellous artist she was? Again, there is no firm answer.

And perhaps in the end it does not matter all that much. She sang what she knew; the deep expressive power of her muse, with its pain and its almost intolerably communicated sense of tainted reality, the drainings of the bitter cup of life, came out of what she knew and only out of that, what she herself had experienced. It does not necessarily have to come that way – as was once argued by the late Eric Blom, a distinguished music critic of his day, that artists do not need personally to experience everything they touch but use the imagination, 'which is the perfect artist's substitute for experience'. No doubt it would be stretching language beyond hyperbole to call Billie Holiday a 'perfect artist', but she was a very good and rarely gifted one. The rest is history, mortal and therefore transitory. What was perishable in her went more than a quarter of a century ago. What is permanent resides in her art, and that, to our great good fortune, is preserved for our enrichment.

For much of her career Billie Holiday had a strange desire to record with strings. I call it strange because her particular voice and, more important, her particular style of singing, seem at odds with the soft cushion of strings. Of course, strings need not always be a soft cushion, but the types of string accompaniment provided for and used by Billie Holiday was precisely that. It might have been different if the strings had been scored by

Stravinsky or Aaron Copland, with suitable asperities of harmony and rhythm. But they were not, and the soft cushion, suggesting the soft option, took precedence. And for Billie Holiday there could be no soft options.

After her recordings for Milt Gabler's Commodore label, she was still technically under contract to Columbia, and their Okeh and Vocalion labels. However, she was able to switch to Decca (American) in 1944, at the instigation of Gabler who had begun his long association with that company. It was with Decca that she began to use a string section in addition to conventional reeds and brass. There have always been those, perhaps a majority, who have felt that Billie Holiday was best served by the backing of a small jazz group, much on the lines of the Wilson-Holiday sessions of the late 1930s. Others, including Miles Davis, argue that she did not ideally need even that, and that all she required was a senstive pianist. She was a good band vocalist, and with bands of the quality of Basie or Ellington she could always shine in a certain way. Her style was essentially intimate, and the small jazz group or solo pianist always suited her best. Just why she harboured that ambition about using strings and maintained it to the end of her life, is another question not easy to answer. It can hardly have been because she was anxious to attract a middlebrow audience, for that would have entailed the kind of artistic compromise she would never tolerate. It must have been something else, something deeper, some profound conviction about herself and her singing. Whatever it was, she was quite passionate about it. Not that she always used strings in the later part of her career; many of the sessions from the mid-1940s onwards are with small jazz groups of varying constitutions, and this applies to most of the recordings she made for Norman Granz during her long contract with him and Jazz at the Philharmonic. All the same, strings continued to dominate her mind and were heavily featured on the last two albums she ever made.

Her Decca recordings were made mostly with Bob Haggart and Toots Camarata as musical directors. Some were done with small groups, even trios, or with other session bands, but the tone was set by these. This meant written out arrangements with a minimum of jazz oriented solos. It might be argued that such a

Ben Webster, Billie Holiday, Johnny Russell, with
Ram Ramrizen (foreground), mid 1960's

Billie Holiday, publicity still when she appeared with
Artie Shaw's Orchestra, 1938

Billie Holiday, publicity shot, early 1940s

Billie Holiday, from the film 'Sound of Jazz'

Arriving in England, 8 February 1954

Max Jones, Louis McKay and Billie, after

r Manchester concert, 12 February 1954

In her dressing room at the Chelsea Palace, 23 February 1959

formula would give her maximum freedom against a formalised backdrop. In one sense it did, but in another it deprived her of one of the jazz musician's greatest allies, the sympathetic response of fellow musicians of equal quality to his or her melodic and harmonic improvisations. With a studio session orchestra this sort of interplay is written out from the beginning. Strings, with their more or less conventional session type scoring and cloying unisons seem to belong to a different world from Billie Holiday's harshly realistic one.

The liking of jazz musicians for playing with strings, a habit that became an epidemic at one time and infected all manner of otherwise righteous jazzmen, including Charlie Parker, Johnny Hodges and Coleman Hawkins, has always been something of a curiosity. One might say that it was a matter of seeking some kind of social and musical respectability, except that many of those who resorted to it were much too intelligent to be accused of that kind of nonsense. In fact Billie Holiday resorted to it several years before it became an epidemic. Whatever the reason, she did it, she meant to do it, and she went on doing it. No use to recall the description by a leading critic – Spike Hughes I think it was – of the Paul Whiteman orchestra as 'lousy with violins'. (She did actually cut one record with Whiteman.)

Whatever one may think of these backings, and the later ones of a similar description, they are certainly good of their kind, and there is no doubt that on some of the tracks Lady sings beautifully. If drug addiction was undermining her physical and mental health, it had not yet shown in her singing. And if it was indeed Joe Guy who started her, well, Joe Guy was present on many of the later Decca sessions infusing a little muted trumpet bop into the proceedings.

4

Fame but small fortune

In the fall of 1946 Billie Holiday went to Hollywood to make her only full length feature film. This was a pretty little piece of historical mush and distortion called *New Orleans*, redeemed in some part by good jazz contributions from Louis Armstrong, Kid Ory, Barney Bigard, Woody Herman, and a few others, plus a course Lady Day in her own inimitable style. On screen she contrived to distinguish herself both by her singing and by her personal appearance, but behind the scenes the production seems to have been beset with difficulties. Predictably, a fair number of these involved Billie Holiday, who was never a patient lady and was seldom prepared to suffer fools at all, let alone gladly, and whose sense of punctuality was erratic, to say the least. But the film, bad though it was both as fiction and as jazz history, did have the useful effect of bringing Billie before a larger popular audience than she had reached before, *Strange Fruit* and strings notwithstanding.

Of course she was cast as a maid. What else could a black girl expect in those days? She took it coolly: 'She's a cute maid!' she told Leonard Feather. But there is no doubt she was disappointed. She never again appeared in a feature film, though whether from her own choice or because she was not asked to is another unanswered question. Her mother had been a maid and had worn herself out in her early days trying to make few ends meet. Billie had seen for herself, both the unrewarding hard labour and the social implications, and she swore she would never do anything like that herself, no matter what the need or temptations. When she was offered the part in *New Orleans* she no doubt smiled a little wryly to herself, however 'cute' the maid. No doubt too she had by the learnt enough lessons in irony to ride it out and over.

After making the film, Billie went straight back to New York and to her job at the Downbeat Club. But nightclub audiences in New York were falling, and after imposing salary cuts all round, including Billie's, the club closed. Instead of looking for another job, she decided to take the private cure for drug addiction which cost plenty and achieved nothing. Then came the Philadelphia bust and her sentence to imprisonment. She was released from Alderson Reformatory after nine months, and immediately made a huge comeback at a Carnegie Hall concert. She was alarmed at the prospect of appearing at so famous a venue and said that the only time in her life when she fainted was after it was over. It was a sell-out and a total success that did much to restore her confidence. At the same time, she decided to look for a new agent. She claimed that her contract with Joe Glaser had run out and she was on the point of deciding to take up with Ed Fishman. Then she changed her mind, but not before Glaser and Fishman had engaged in a public row which brought Billie more notoriety but also more professional complications since for a time no one knew who her real agent was.

Despite her drug addiction, Billie's physical appearance during these years was something to remember. She had developed into a strikingly beautiful woman with a natural grace and elegance, one to whom the sobriquet Lady Day seemed unusually appropriate. For the most part she looked a million and frequently sounded it even if she did not always feel it. Her skin in particular had a wonderful sheen, but then as Diana Vreeland remarked 'I've never seen anyone on drugs who didn't have a wonderful skin.' Her habits of unpunctuality persisted and continued to get her into trouble, as when she fell out with the management of Chicago's Silhouette Club where she was supposed to be the star turn with a band led by Jimmy McPartland.

Trouble dogged her. Back in California at the beginning of 1949 she was involved in a fracas at Billy Berg's club when she accused someone of trying to molest her and then found herself arrested on a narcotics charge. This was her time with John Levy, and although she saw him as a true friend and although he too was arrested and charged, the relationship was fraught and had no aspect of permanence. Both Levy and Lady were acquitted, eventually, the jury believing that Billie had been framed by Levy on the drugs charge, as she herself claimed. It had however the effect of putting more pressure on her, especially when her attorney, Jacob W. Ehrlich, started demanding settlement of his fee. She still could not get her New York cabaret card although she made a formal appeal to the court for its return, the judge not only turned her down but actually commended the police authorities for having refused it in the first place.

Although she hit a new low, she was never one to go down without a fight. She was still caught up in the California rap when the judge made his ruling, but began to play to theatre audiences, though this was not her proper venue, and in clubs outside New York City, notably at the Blue Note in Chicago. By all accounts she was singing well, though she often appeared to be in poor physical shape. Even so, not everyone thought she was on top form even as a singer. Mike Levin wrote in *Downbeat* during 1949 that there were limits to the distortion a singer can inflict on a good song and Billie Holiday had reached and passed them. It was probably no consolation to her – and in any case she would not have known – that it was the kind of charge often levelled against performers in other fields and was a one also frequently laid against so distinguished a figure as Wilhelm Furtwängler. In fact, the legend of Billie Holiday's 'decline' had begun and the insidious process of always referring back to her pre-1940 work to find the real Billie Holiday had already raised its ugly little head. She was still making records, but they were not achieving notable success. Because of her reputation for drug addiction disc-jockeys and other promoters in the popular mass media left her in the cold. They were not enthusiastic anyway. A pure jazz singer like Lady Day was for connoisseurs and had no mass appeal.

But in clubs she was still a top performer, and around this time she appeared at George Wein's Storyville Club where she shared the bill with Stan Getz's group. One or two of their joint performances have found their way onto somewhat dim and distant but still revealing records.

She had long wanted to tour England and Europe, and in the autumn of 1952 it looked as though she was set to realise that ambition. By that time her new husband, Louis NcKay, who she had first met in 1935 and re-met and married in 1951, was also her manager. At first it seemed as though she had at last found personal happiness. Of course it was not to be: her second marriage came unstuck like the first one and like all the affairs and relationships in between. But before that, and for a time while it lasted, a kind of happiness did make a tentative entry into her life.

Unfortunately, and to her great chagrin, the proposed tour was cancelled. She continued club and theatre engagements, with radio and television appearances thrown in. She still had no police cabaret card, she could not work the club circuit in New York, but elsewhere she could and did. Oddly, in view of her fame and experience, she was still menacingly subject to first night nerves, especially on and before the big occasion. There is no doubt too that although she could still reach the top as a singer, and frequently did, her health was now beginning to deteriorate as a result of her addictions. Also, she remained convinced that the Federal narcotics agents were still after her, and this in itself contributed to her sense of insecurity. In fact they were probably not bothering. If they had wanted to, they could have picked her up any time.

If the abortive tour to Europe in 1952 had been a big disappointment, in early 1954 it was reversed when she was invited to tour with a package arranged by the critic Leonard Feather going by the title 'Jazz Club U.S.A.'. It is doubtful if any arrangement in the whole of Billie Holiday's life was without problems, and this one was no exception. For her, even the normally straightforward business of obtaining a passport was widely complicated and apart from causing headaches all round, at one time very nearly caused her participation in the tour to be in jeopardy. The trouble was not so much her record of brushes with the law as the curious anomaly that she could not produce a birth certificate. The circumstances of her birth, so splendidly (if perhaps apocryphally) described in that famous opening paragraph of her autobiography, had the effect that she never had a birth certificate of any kind and there was no possibility of obtaining one. Since it must have been obvious even to the obtuse official mind that she had been born and definitely existed, the difficulty might be thought to have been more formal than real. But logic and the official mind do not often cohabit, so it became necessary for someone to stand guarantor for her, presumably as surety that Billie Holiday lived and was who she said she was. In the end, it was her stepmother, Clarence Holiday's official second wife, who performed that necessary office. So at the end of the day all was well and Lady Day set off for Stockholm with her current accompanist, Carl Drinkard, and the other groups that made up the package, including those led by Red Norvo, Buddy de Franco and Beryl Bryden.

On the whole, after initial problems the tour was a considerable success, not least for Billie Holiday herself. Louis McKay went with her and helped smooth a few rough paths, though they were never all that rough in the first place. The least successful part was probably the English end. To begin with, because of the quarrelling between the musicians' union in England and America, the same quarrelling that kept the Duke Ellington orchestra out of the country between their first visit in 1933 and their second in 1958, the whole package could not appear in England. Only Billie Holiday and Carl Drinkard of the musicians could come, plus Leonard Feather and Louis McKay, on the 'one for one' ruling that prevailed at the time. Secondly, at a press conference she was confronted with journalists who knew nothing about music and cared less and whose only interest was in the sensational aspects of Billie Holiday's life, and the amount of cheap copy they could screw out of it. It threw her at first, as they lobbed a barrage of questions about her narcotics involvement. Then Max Jones of the *Melody Maker* moved in, silenced the sensation mongers, and directed his own questions to her career and her musical colleagues. At once she relaxed, came off the defensive, talked freely and generously about her art and those musicians she had known and worked with, and as a consequence found in Max a good friend for the rest of her life.

If the British press and aspects of British officialdom did what they could to sour the visit, the British public warmed to her and gave her a magnificent reception, over 6000 of them at the Royal Albert Hall alone.

But despite her success and the esteem in which she was held by public and musicians alike in England and most of Europe, there was still a deep running vein of sadness in her life. She had long ago said good-morning to heartache, and it was to be her loyal companion until death took its place.

Back in the States she carried on as before. She had a varied schedule of work to do, and she did it. Mostly she did it well, though there were increasing times when her physical and mental stability were clearly undermined. There were reunions with people she had known and worked with in her early days, notably with Teddy Wilson and Lester Young. Of course it was not as it had been before. It never is or can be. The intervening years had wrought changes in everybody, and however much they may have wished to short-circuit time and recapture the halcyon days, they are always reluctant to return, in any form. Perhaps the knowledge of how time had passed and how far off were those days of pristine achievement, served in some way to increase her depression and her sadness. By now she had been under contract to Norman Granz for some time, and it was Granz who was responsible for many of her best later recordings, in the long Verve series which appeared originally between 1952 and 1958. She had recorded for Granz, via J.A.T.P., since 1946; but from 1952 Granz had total control over her work in the studio and ensured that she had the backing for true jazz musicians who could do her justice.

Her standing as a singer remained stable, despite those occasions when for one reason or another she could not give of her best, but she still did not take top honours in the national polls. She never won either the *Downbeat* or the *Metronome* critics' polls, being invariably topped by Ella Fitzgerald and Sarah Vaughan and some times coming way down the lists. This of course in no way reflected the state of her art in any one year. It was simply further confirmation that she was always a connoisseur's singer and that only the privileged few really understood the full subtleties and the uniqueness of her singing. It caused her disappointment, this lack of official recognition, but she had long learned to accept that it would be so, apparently as long ago as the Artie Shaw days. Some consolation did come when *Downbeat* made a special award for her in 1954 as 'one of the all-time great vocalists in jazz'. She was more put out by the treatment she received from the Negro press, which frequently ignored her or concerned themselves like other low grade journalists with only her extra-musical problems. It hurt her for she was proud of being black and she thought she had a right to expect better from her own people. In particular, she expected some serious consideration of her singing and what it meant in both the social and the musical context of the times. No doubt part of it was again her own fault; no doubt some at least of the editors and journalists thought that by getting herself so often into the news the way she did and being involved with narcotics she was letting the side down, and bringing the whole Negro race into disrepute. A little public support from her own people might have been a major help, and some attention to her art from the same source could have reassured her that even if the larger public and the major white press did not understand her, her own people did. It was perhaps asking too much: for newsmongers to attend to art rather than narcotics runs altogether against the grain, as was amply demonstrated to her in England.

Another habit of critics and journalists that annoyed and depressed her in her later years was their increasing way of holding up her past work as the touchstone by which she should be judged. More and more she felt isolated and unappreciated; and after the breakup of her marriage to Louis McKay her depression inevitably deepened. At several periods in her life she said that all she wanted was to settle down with her man; latterly just to be a good wife and make a home for Mr McKay. It was not a unique wish, and many have doubted if she really meant what she said. But sometimes artists do feel persecuted by their talent and is often pitiless demands.

Whatever her real wishes in that direction, it was not to be for Billie Holiday. Exactly why she and Louis McKay split is not clear. There does not seem to have been any specific reason or cause, even a decisive trigger. More than anything it appears to have been a case of growing incompatibility leading to increasing quarrels. It was now 1957, and Billie still had periods when she was in good fighting trim. But increasing alcoholism added to heroin addiction was progressively undermining her health and was reflected in her vocal powers. The previous year, 1956, she had been arrested, again in Philadelphia, on a narcotics charge. At the same time, Louis McKay was arraigned on a charge of possessing a pistol without a licence. Billie wrote that McKay claimed he had left the gun on the top layer of his suitcase where it was sure to be found, if they were searched, in the hope that it would divert police attention from finding drugs. They were both released on bail, but the pattern of Lady Day's life was not showing any noticeable changes.

She herself believed that she was singing better than ever and some musicians, like Miles Davis, have agreed with her, finding a depth and maturity lacking from her earlier work. Whatever may have been the case when she was on top form, it is clear that she was becoming more and more erratic. The quality of her tone was losing its resonance, she was having increasing problems with her pitching, and her melodic reshapings were often mannered, sometimes even eccentric, in a way she would never have permitted herself in her prime. The deterioration in the quality of her voice, could not be hidden and only to a small extent disguised. One often thought that towards the end of his life her old crony Lester Young was reduced to using his horn to mumble his despair. With Billie Holiday the impression remains that she would often croak her defiance as well as her unhappiness. Yet the results were curiously similar. In both cases, sudden late flowerings of the true worth became all the more poignant.

The summer of 1956 was a time of some relief from the mounting gloom of her life. Her autobiography, '*Lady Sings the Blues*', written in collaboration with William Dufty, was published in the States, and in that July she made one of the best of her late albums, '*Songs for Distingué Lovers*', with the kind of small jazz group that suited her so well – Harry Edison (t), Ben Webster (ts), Jimmy Rowles (p), Barney Kessel (g), Alvin Stoller or Larry Bunker (d). These men were all sympathetic collaborators. She had worked before with Edison and Webster, and Rowles was her accompanist on many occasions and a trusted friend. This is late Holiday of a quality that makes one almost weep for what might have been in the years to come had things gone differently with her. Late in 1956 came the famous celebration at Carnegie Hall at which Billie sang in two sessions, one with Carl Drinkard and Kenny Burrell (g), Carl Smith (b), Chico Hamilton (d), plus Roy Eldridge (t) and Coleman

Hawkins (ts), the other with Buck Clayton (t) and Tony Scott (cl & p). Between numbers Gilbert Milstein read extracts from the book. Parts of the concert, including some of the readings, were recorded and commercially issued. Billie was generally in good form. It was not without moments of anxiety for her and her voice, but overall the occasion was successful.

1958 was not a good year. In retrospect it can be seen as the beginning of the end. Another trip to Europe was planned but aborted on account of the political situation in France over Algeria. She was not only disappointed but also lost work because she had cancelled engagements to make the trip. She seriously considered emigrating to England permanently. She liked the place and the people, and she had it seriously in mind to settle there. As usual with her hopes, plans and aspirations, nothing came of it, but ever since many have claimed that if she had made the move she might have lived into reasonable old age and continued to sing her way towards it, to everyone's benefit, her own most of all.

Her last two albums were made in association with Ray Ellis whose studio-type orchestra, replete with strings, so appealed to her that she specially requested the setup. Although she herself thought the first fruits of this collaboration, '*Lady in Satin*', one of her best records, the results were in fact depressing. Her voice lacked the old richness and resonance, at times her sense of musical direction sounded suspect, and the feeling that too often she is croaking out an inescapable despair is hard to resist. Nor is the setting worthy of her, and she was less able to counter it now that her old assurance was all but gone. But the real clue to one's discomfort probably comes as much as anything from the combination of Billie Holiday and Ray Ellis. She had been attracted to Ellis's work by the scores he wrote for something called 'Ellis in Wonderland', and that is the clue. The Ellis type of music was indeed a kind of Wonderland fantasy, a dreamy never-never land a thousand miles removed from the hard, tough, uncompromising world of the real Billie Holiday. If she really thought '*Lady in Satin*' among her best recordings, she either deceived herself or her judgment had faded along with her other attributes. The last record of all she did not like so much. Perhaps on her deathbed, where she lay when the test pressing were sent to her, her self-assessment reasserted itself. This has a mixture of the Ellis orchestral background and a small group of good jazz musicians. According to Leonard Feather who was present at the sessions, Lady Day was in good shape at the time. She turned up dressed with her old familiar elegance and style, and was in generally alert nick. But the voice had gone, however much she may have been in condition to use it well. It is a better album than '*Lady in Satin*', despite her own view of the matter, but it is still full of communicated pain.

She did ultimately tour Europe again for a last time, with her final accompanist, Mal Waldron. It was a tour of mixed fortunes and caused her some disappointment, exaggerated by the eagerness with which she had looked forward to it. She visited London briefly early in 1959, for a television appearance, but it was clear that the sands were running out for her. This seemed to be confirmed when she returned to the States and found bookings few and mostly unsatisfactory. Her reputation for being both vocally and personally unreliable and unpredictable was by now common knowledge among agents and impressarios, and she was obliged to accept engagements in places in no way worthy of her and her talent. More and more, too, she withdrew into herself, spent her evenings when she was not working alone in her apartment, watching television or listening to records. Friends who visited her became fewer as her moods became increasingly depressive. At last, on the final day of May, she collapsed and was taken to hospital. At first a heroin OD was suspected as the primary cause, but in fact no evidence for it was found. She did not suffer withdrawal symptoms, and it seemed that she had been off heroin for some time. Her condition was diagnosed as cirrhosis of the liver leading to cardiac failure. To this was soon added the even more dangerous condition of kidney disease. She responded to treatment at first, but it was clear to everyone that she would have to be more than lucky to survive.

And to the end the police continued to harrass her. They searched her in her hospital bed, claimed to have found a small package of heroin on her person, and charged her with possession. Since she was too ill to be moved, a police guard was placed outside her door. Whatever the final truth about the package, whether it was a plant or was given her by some well meaning but misguided admirer, has never been satisfactorily explained. Where the police claimed to have found it makes it almost certain that she could not have put it there herself. But the irony remains.

She had filed for divorce from Louis McKay in 1958. But she still retained his name and was admitted to hospital as Eleanora McKay. When he heard the news of her illness, Louis McKay flew in from California, and after Billie's death he was declared her sole legatee.

The end came on 17 July 1959. Two days earlier she had received the last rites of the Catholic Church, her mother's faith having at least nominally stayed with her to the last day of her life. After her death the sum of $750 was found strapped to her leg. Always suspicious of official institutions, she was taking no chances: her bank balance showed a credit of 75c.

She hoped all the time that she would recover. She knew that when she came out of hospital she would have to face a narcotics charge yet again. But her defiance remained: whatever else may have been left to her of health and aspiration, her courage was intact. One can easily imagine that among her last gestures would have been a sardonic grin at the thought of policeman keeping watch in the corridor outside, and among her last words one of her famous expletives at their expense, knowing that she would soon be beyond their greedy reach. The precise cause of her death is not defined. Perhaps it is best to remember the words of a man who, when asked the cause of Bix Beiderbecke's death, replied, simply and honestly: 'Everything'.

Four months before her own death Billie Holiday had attended the funeral of Lester Young. As she walked away she gave an indication of her frame of mind when she said to a companion: 'It'll be me next.' And to the end the parallels remained. It could be said that Lester Young more or less committed suicide. Much the same might be said of Billie Holiday; certainly the urge towards self-destruction was strong in her, however much (and however paradoxically) she may have wanted, and tried, to counter it. She made her own end. But in spite of that, there can be no possible doubt that for her as for Lester, American racism set her up for it.

The Summing Up

Restraint was one of the secrets of her art, restraint and a subtle way of penetrating to the emotional core of a song. She did not need the rhetorical gesture, the metaphorical bearing of the breast for public exhibition. As a singer she had no need to resort to the 'can belto' style widely favoured among many of her successors in popular song. She sang in an intimate manner which suggested that she was communicating directly with each one of her auditors, personally and individually. On stage she did not jump about and wave her arms, tear her hair or rend her garments in an effort to convince her audience of her unimpeachable sincerity. She would stand as she sang almost still, the familiar white gardenia in her hair, only a slight rocking from the hips and sometimes a snapping of the fingers as carefully timed as her handling of the beat and her accentuating of the melody: it was never a mere adjunct, a superfluity, but always related to the totality of the performance.

Those who never saw and heard Billie Holiday 'in the flesh' – and their number is inevitably increasing – are obliged to make a number of assumptions and to take a certain amount on trust. To be obliged to rely on recordings, especially those of not the most modern vintage and technical sophistication, is to begin at a disadvantage. Though much can be deduced, the general style appreciated, even in many cases the personal presence felt, the tone must always be to a greater or lesser extent an approximation. Despite the enormous advances in recording techniques, even today the finest points of vocal and instrumental tones have to be deduced rather than received directly. But Billie Holiday did not live into the age of advanced digital stereo recording, compact discs, and all the rest. Many of her albums, especially the later ones, are of good technical quality, but the early ones in particular, those which preserve her partnership with Lester Young, however carefully re-mastered, have inherent limitations, and represent a kind of blueprint or groundplan from which the nature and reality of the edifice can be deduced by exercise of the imagination.

All this is relevant to a discussion of Billie Holiday partly because like all artists of an older musical generation she can now only be assessed via recordings, and secondly because her art was so intimate, so personal, so dependent on person to person communication that one might at first suppose that too much would be lost in the process of transmission. One might also well assume that the more objective kind of artist, the accomplished virtuoso performer, would be most likely to transcend the limitations of the recording studio and recorded sound; but in fact it is by no means always so: intimate art in fact makes the transition as well as any other.

Billie Holiday's art was essentially intimate. She recognised it herself; her ambition to have her own club and so create the conditions she needed as well as the freedom to sing as she wanted to, was not simply a private conceit. It was a conscious recognition of the nature of her art. She could sing before big crowds in big halls, just as she could sing in front of a big band. And in each case she could make a tremendous impression. But it was not her natural venue nor her right audience. At her best, and in her proper setting, each song that she sang became a miniature transformation scene. These essence of her communicative power was, like the quality of her voice, best deployed on a fairly restricted scale

Both the strength and the fallibility of her art were rooted deep inside her. It is doubtful if any major jazz artist was so beset by inconsistency, and as time went by and the life she led bit more damagingly into her, the fallibility increased. Her failures could assume tragic proportions. A bad record, even a merely indifferent one, by most singers can be dealt with, sold off or stored away on some shelf out of harm's way, but a bad record by Billie Holiday caused genuine pain, like the opening of an old wound. Her failures could communicate as tellingly as her successes, sometimes more so. It was, as it so often is in the case of truly subjective artists whose appeal depends primarily on direct communication, a price that had to be paid for the potency of her true successes. Today what is usually referred to as 'communication' is more likely to be called 'identification', not quite accurately, or rather it is not quite the same thing. To 'identify' in this sense is to miss the real point of a true communication; the most profound communicators are those who touch a universal rather than a personal response, who work that is can be, indeed demands to be, received with a major element of objectivity. With a singer whose art is so essentially subjective, this may seem a contradiction, and so in a sense it is; yet the real implication is that it is the core of the paradox of which I have already spoken. It is closely related to the objective-subjective balance, itself a kind of paradox, which lies at the heart of all art which aspires to transcend the obvious and the commonplace, in whatever field or area.

She was uncompromising in everything, and she paid the price in several different currencies. She was almost too honest. Just as she would not sing any other way than her own, the way she knew was right for her and determined to do no other, even at risk of loss of engagements, quarrels with agents and impresarios, even with musical colleagues, so she would not live any other way. That she was frequently obstinate, pig-headed to her own detriment is too obvious to need further elucidation. She would probably have admitted it herself. But she remained true to her own determination not to say anything unless she meant it and to say what she meant without fear or favour. And if she paid for it, in the end with her life, she would almost certainly have accepted the price. She confronted life with a challenge that was both courageous and reckless. Over the years it tore ragged holes in her, and out of the wounds flowed both the greatness and the vulnerability of her art. From the worst possible beginnings she picked up the gauntlet, accepted the gambit and out of it fashioned an art of popular song that has spread its influence everywhere. If sometimes her influence has been less than healthy, that is inevitable.

The art that she fashioned had many unique characteristics. It is always difficult to describe in words the precise elements which go to the making of a musical sound or style, especially the sound. And sound is perhaps the first thing about Billie Holiday's singing that catches the ear – that and her highly personal phrasing. She could turn a melody so that the common-place suddenly began to sound like the unique, and if it was a distinguished melody in the first place, then she would subtly add to that distinction by her treatment of it. But she never at her best treated a tune with contempt – at least not with public contempt, whatever may have been her private view of it. One of the most familiar devices she used to impress her particular style on a song and by so doing extend its range and scope was the way she would lag behind the beat and then suddenly come down on it in a way that made of momentarily forget she had ever lagged at all. It might be tempting to say that she pounced on the beat from behind, as it were, at exactly the point in the song and its performance when it was required; but in fact, like all true artists she would often make the pounce when the listener (and the song) was least expecting it. That was another reason why she so particularly needed sympathetic accompanists, and why her partnership with Lester Young was so memorable. They thought and felt uncannily alike, those two, and the result was unmatched anywhere in popular music and only rarely equalled in any area of music.

Every true style, the style which goes beyond style, is an accurate reflection of the person who creates it. No more than emotion itself can a true style be created at second hand. A shrewd comment by critic and writer Benny Green sums it up: 'Billie Holiday's great performances are the fruit of her experiences of her own life. The performances of her imitators are the fruit of their experience of Billie Holiday.'

APPENDIX I

'Lady sings the Blues'

The book:

Critics and musicians who were around at the time have made play with the evident exaggerations and errors of detail. Certainly Billie Holiday's memory was by no means infallible; and certainly she was not particular about whom she offended and what toes she trod on. But none of this matters. The book, however she and her collaboratory, William Dufty, may have intended it, is not a factual record or a catalogue of events. It is the record of a life told from the inside. It tells us, beyond all the critical commentaries and appreciations, excellent though some of them are, beyond the minutae of biography, what Billie Holiday felt and thought about Billie Holiday. That is its real value – and as such it is both absorbing and irreplaceable. It has been called bitter and sour. In view in the circumstances of her life and how she was treated by the world's riff-raff with whom she allowed herself to consort, it has always struck me a unusually mild. Naturally, it aroused resentment in some quarters, disbelief in others; but then the world never does like someone who stands up and says what she thinks and means, whether she is black and poor or white and rich or any permutation of categories. Whoever and whatever you are, to stand up and say what you think and mean it is the surest way to get knocked on the head. The book is more honest than many of its critics and detractors.

The film:

Predictably, it wallowed in the motif of drug addiction, and skated feebly and ignorantly over the musical aspects. Only the vaguest and uninterested mentions of the musicians who were important to her and her work; virtually none at all of Lester Young. Diana Ross wisely did not attempt to reproduce the true Billie Holiday tone and style. She sang reasonably well in a role which was fundamentally impossible. But for the sensational element introduced by the drug problem, no one would have thought it worth making in the first place. As it was, it remains what it always purported to be – a piece of cheap sensationalism nominally based on the life of a great jazz singer.

During her lifetime several suggestions for making a film about her were put forward. She would have liked to see it done, but was apprehensive about the outcome. Several names were put forward as possibles to play her on the screen; to most she objected strongly, over the rest she had more apprehensions. How right she was is indicated by what eventually did come out of the Hollywood machine. It could have been so much better, done her memory so much more justice. It is impossible to say it might have been better. There was never the remotest chance that it would be. To tell the truth in such a case would have been box office death. As it was, it was perhaps the final exploitation of a woman who was ruthlessly exploited all her short life.

Billie Holiday
A SELECTIVE DISCOGRAPHY

I have based my selections on records generally available at the time of going to press and further listening suggestions follow the main discography. Limitations of space have made it necessary to use the following abbreviations (arr) arrangement; (as) alto sax; (b) bass; (bars) baritone sax; (cl) clarinet; (d) drums; (fl) flute; (g) guitar; (p) piano; (sop) soprano sax; (tb) trombone; (tp) trumpet; (ts) tenor sax; any other instruments are given in full. Only records issued in (Eu) Europe and (Am) United States of America are noted. I would like to thank Alan F. Newby, Billie Holiday researcher for his assistance.

TONY MIDDLETON *London, January 1984*

BILLIE HOLIDAY (vocal) on all titles.

BENNY GOODMAN AND HIS ORCHESTRA:
Charlie Teagarden, Shirley Clay (tp); Jack Teagarden (tb); Benny Goodman
(cl); Arthur Karle (ts); Joe Sullivan (p); Dick McDonough (g); Artie Bernstein
(b); Gene Krupa (d). *NYC. November 27, 1933.*

W152568-3 YOUR MOTHER'S SON-IN-LAW		CBS(Eu)68228,
		Columbia(Am)PG32121
W152568-3		*NYC. December 18, 1933*
W152650-2 RIFFIN' THE SCOTCH		CBS(Eu)68228,
		Columbia(Am)PG32121

TEDDY WILSON AND HIS ORCHESTRA:
Roy Eldridge (tp); Ben Webster (ts); Teddy Wilson (p); John Truehart (g); John
Kirby (b); Cozy Cole (d). *NYC. July 2, 1935*

B17769-1 A SUNBONNET BLUE		CBS(Eu)68229,
		Columbia(Am)PG32124

TEDDY WILSON AND HIS ORCHESTRA:
Roy Eldridge (tp); Cecil Scott (cl); Hilton Jefferson (as); Ben Webster (ts);
Teddy Wilson (p); Lawrence Lucie (g); John Kirby (b); Cozy Cole (d). *NYC.
July 31, 1935*

B17913-1 WHAT A NIGHT, WHAT A		CBS(Eu)68229,
MOON, WHAT A GIRL		Columbia(Am)PG32124
B17914-1 I'M PAINTING THE TOWN RED		CBS(Eu)68229,
		Columbia(Am)PG32124
B17915-1 IT'S TOO HOT FOR WORDS		CBS(Eu)68229,
		Columbia(Am)PG32124

TEDDY WILSON AND HIS ORCHESTRA:
Dick Clark (tp); Tom Mace (cl); Johnny Hodges (as); Teddy Wilson (p); Dave
Barbour (g); Grachan Moncur (b); Cozy Cole (d). *NYC. December 3, 1935.*

B18318-1 YOU LET ME DOWN		CBS(Eu)68229,
		Columbia(Am)PG32124

TEDDY WILSON AND HIS ORCHESTRA:
Jonah Jones (tp); Johnny Hodges (as); Harry Carney (cl,bars); Teddy Wilson
(p); Lawrence Lucie (g); John Kirby (b); Cozy Cole (d). *NYC. June 30, 1936.*

B19495-2 IT'S LIKE REACHING		CBS(Eu)68229,
FOR THE MOON		Columbia(Am)PG32124
B19496-2 THESE FOOLISH THINGS		CBS(Eu)68228,
		Columbia(Am)PG32121

BILLIE HOLIDAY AND HER ORCHESTRA:
Bunny Berigan (tp); Artie Shaw (cl); Joe Bushkin (p); Dick McDonough (g);
Pete Peterson (b); Cozy Cole (d) *NYC. July 30, 1936*

| B19535-1 | DID I REMEMBER? | CBS(Eu)68228, Columbia(Am)PG32121 |
| B19536-1 | NO REGRETS | CBS(Eu)68228, Columbia(Am)PG32121 |

BILLIE HOLIDAY AND HER ORCHESTRA:
Bunny Berigan (tp); Irving Fazola (cl); Clyde Hart (p); Dick McDonough (g);
Artie Bernstein (b); Cozy Cole (d). *NYC. September 29, 1936*

| B19971-1 | A FINE ROMANCE | CBS(Eu)68228, Columbia(Am)PG32121 |

TEDDY WILSON AND HIS ORCHESTRA:
Irving Randolph (tp); Vido Musso (cl); Ben Webster (ts); Teddy Wilson (p);
Allen Reuss (g); Milt Hinton (b); Gene Krupa (d). *NYC. October 20, 1936.*

| B20105-1 | EASY TO LOVE | CBS(Eu)68228, Columbia(Am)PG32121 |
| B20107-2 | THE WAY YOU LOOK TONIGHT | CBS(Eu)68228, Columbia(Am)PG32121 |

TEDDY WILSON AND HIS ORCHESTRA:
Jonah Jones (tp); Benny Goodman (cl); Ben Webster (ts); Teddy Wilson (p);
Allen Reuss (g); John Kirby (b); Cozy Cole (d). *NYC. November 19, 1936.*

B20290-1	PENNIES FROM HEAVEN	CBS(Eu)68228, Columbia(Am)PG32121
B20291-1	THAT'S LIFE I GUESS	CBS(Eu)68228, Columbia(Am)PG32121
B20293-1	I CAN'T GIVE YOU ANYTHING BUT LOVE	CBS(Eu)68228, Columbia(Am)PG32121

BILLIE HOLIDAY AND HER ORCHESTRA:
Jonah Jones (tp); Edgar Sampson (cl,as); Ben Webster (ts); Teddy Wilson (p);
Allen Reuss (g); John Kirby (b); Cozy Cole (d). *NYC. January 12, 1937.*

| B20506-1 | ONE NEVER KNOWS DOES ONE? | CBS(Eu)68229, Columbia(Am)PG32124 |
| B20507-1 | I'VE GOT MY LOVE TO KEEP ME WARM | CBS(Eu)68229, Columbia(Am)PG32124 |

TEDDY WILSON AND HIS ORCHESTRA:

Buck Clayton (tp); Benny Goodman (cl); Lester Young (ts); Teddy Wilson (p); Freddie Green (g); Walter Page (b); Jo Jones (d). *NYC. January 25, 1937*

| B20569-2 | THIS YEAR'S KISSES | CBS(Eu)68228, Columbia(Am)PG32121 |
| B20570-1 | WHY WAS I BORN? | CBS(Eu)68228, Columbia(Am)PG32121 |

TEDDY WILSON AND HIS ORCHESTRA:

Red Allen (tp); Cecil Scott (cl,as); Prince Robinson (ts); Teddy Wilson (p); Jimmy McLin (g); John Kirby (b); Cozy Cole (d). *NYC. February 18, 1937*

B20698-2	THE MOOD THAT I'M IN	CBS(Eu)68228, Columbia(Am)PG32121
B20699-2	YOU SHOWED ME THE WAY	CBS(Eu)68229, Columbia(Am)PG32124
B20700-2	SENTIMENTAL AND MELANCHOLY	CBS(Eu)68229, Columbia(Am)PG32124
B20701-1	MY LAST AFFAIR	CBS(Eu)68229, Columbia(Am)PG32124

TEDDY WILSON AND HIS ORCHESTRA:

Cootie Williams (tp); Johnny Hodges (as); Harry Carney (cl,bars); Teddy Wilson (p); Allen Reuss (g); John Kirby (b); Cozy Cole (d). *NYC. March 31, 1937.*

B20911-3	CARELESSLY	CBS(Eu)68229, Columbia(Am)PG32124
B20912-1	HOW COULD YOU	CBS(Eu)68229, Columbia(Am)PG32124
B20913-1	MOANIN' LOW	CBS(Eu)68229, Columbia(Am)PG32124

BILLIE HOLIDAY AND HER ORCHESTRA:

Eddie Tompkins (tp); Buster Bailey (cl); Joe Thomas (ts); Teddy Wilson (p); Carmen Mastren (g); John Kirby (b); Alphonse Steele (d). *NYC. April 1, 1937.*

| B20918-1 | WHERE IS THE SUN | CBS(Eu)68229, Columbia(Am)PG32124 |
| B20919-1 | LET'S CALL THE WHOLE THING OFF | CBS(Eu)68229, Columbia(Am)PG32124 |

74

TEDDY WILSON AND HIS ORCHESTRA:

Buck Clayton (tp); Buster Bailey (cl); Johnny Hodges (as); Lester Young (ts); Teddy Wilson (p); Allen Reuss (g); Artie Bernstein (b); Cozy Cole (d). *NYC. May 11, 1937*

B21117-2	SUN SHOWERS – 1	CBS(Eu)68230, Columbia(Am)PG32127
B21119-1	I'LL GET BY	CBS(Eu)68230, Columbia(Am)PG32127
B21120-1	MEAN TO ME	CBS(Eu)68230, Columbia(Am)PG32127

– 1 Barney Bigard (cl) replaces Buster Bailey.

TEDDY WILSON AND HIS ORCHESTRA

Buck Clayton (tp); Buster Bailey (cl); Lester Young (ts); Teddy Wilson (p); Freddie Green (g); Walter Page (b); Jo Jones (d). *NYC. June 1, 1937*

B21219-2	I'LL NEVER BE THE SAME˙	CBS(Eu)68228, Columbia(Am)PG32121

BILLIE HOLIDAY AND HER ORCHESTRA:

Buck Clayton (tp); Edmond Hall (cl); Lester Young (ts); James Sherman (p); Freddie Green (g); Walter Page (b); Jo Jones (d). *NYC. June 15, 1937*

B21252-1	WITHOUT YOUR LOVE	CBS(Eu)68228, Columbia(Am)PG32121

COUNT BASIE AND HIS ORCHESTRA:

Ed Lewis, Bobby Moore, Buck Clayton (tp); Dan Minor, George Hunt (tb); Earl Warren (as); Lester Young (cl,ts); Herschel Evans (ts); Jack Washington (bars); Count Basie (p); Freddie Green (g); Walter Page (b); Jo Jones (d). *"Radio broadcast", Savoy Ballroom. NYC. June 30, 1937*

SWING, BROTHER SWING	CBS(Eu)68228, Columbia(Am)PG32121
THEY CAN'T TAKE THAT AWAY FROM ME	CBS(Eu)68228, Columbia(Am)PG32121

BILLIE HOLIDAY AND HER ORCHESTRA:

Buck Clayton (tp); Buster Bailey (cl); Lester Young (ts); Claude Thornhill (p); Freddie Green (g); Walter Page (b); Jo Jones (d). *NYC. September 13, 1937.*

B21686-1	GETTING SOME FUN OUT OF LIFE	CBS(Eu)68228, Columbia(Am)PG32121
B21688-1	TRAV'LIN' ALL ALONE	CBS(Eu)68228, Columbia(Am)PG32121
B21689-1	HE'S FUNNY THAT WAY	CBS(Eu)68230, Columbia(Am)PG32127

TEDDY WILSON AND HIS ORCHESTRA:

Buck Clayton (tp); Prince Robinson, Vido Musso (cl,ts); Teddy Wilson (p); Allen Reuss (g); Walter Page (b); Cozy Cole (d). *NYC. November 1, 1937*

B21982-1	NICE WORK IF YOU CAN GET IT	CBS(Eu)68230, Columbia(Am)PG32127
B21984-1	MY MAN	CBS(Eu)68230, Columbia(Am)PG32127
B21985-1	CAN'T HELP LOVIN' DAT MAN	CBS(Eu)68230, Columbia(Am)PG32127

COUNT BASIE AND HIS ORCHESTRA:

Ed Lewis, Bobby Moore, Buck Clayton (tp); Dan Minor, Benny Morton (tb); Earl Warren (as); Lester Young (cl,ts); Herschel Evans (ts); Jack Washington (bars); Count Basie (p); Freddie Green (g); Walter Page (b); Jo Jones (d); Eddie Durham (g,tb). *"Radio broadcast" Meadowbrook Ballroom. New Jersey. November 3, 1937*

| | I CAN'T GET STARTED | CBS(Eu)68228, Columbia(Am)PG32121 |

TEDDY WILSON AND HIS ORCHESTRA:

Buck Clayton (tp); Benny Morton (tb); Lester Young (ts); Teddy Wilson (p); Freddie Green (g); Walter Page (b); Jo Jones (d). *NYC. January 6, 1938*

B22192-4	MY FIRST IMPRESSION OF YOU	CBS(Eu)68230, Columbia(Am)PG32127
B22194-3	WHEN YOU'RE SMILING	CBS(Eu)68228, Columbia(Am)PG32121
B22195-4	I CAN'T BELIEVE THAT YOU'RE IN LOVE WITH ME	CBS(Eu)68230, Columbia(Am)PG32127
B22255-1	IF DREAMS COME TRUE	CBS(Eu)68228, Columbia(Am)PG32121

BILLIE HOLIDAY AND HER ORCHESTRA:

Buck Clayton (tp); Benny Morton (tb); Lester Young (ts); Teddy Wilson (p); Freddie Green (g); Walter Page (b); Jo Jones (d). *NYC. January 12, 1938*

B22281-2	NOW THEY CALL IT SWING	CBS(Eu)68230, Columbia(Am)PG32127
B22282-1	ON THE SENTIMENTAL SIDE	CBS(Eu)68228, Columbia(Am)PG32121
B22283-1	BACK IN YOUR OWN BACKYARD	CBS(Eu)68228, Columbia(Am)PG32121
B22284-1	WHEN A WOMAN LOVES A MAN	CBS(Eu)68228, Columbia(Am)PG32121

BILLIE HOLIDAY AND HER ORCHESTRA:

Bernard Anderson (tp); Buster Bailey (cl); Babe Russin (ts); Claude Thornhill (p); John Kirby (b); Cozy Cole (d). *NYC. May 11, 1938*

| B22921-1 | YOU GO TO MY HEAD | CBS(Eu)68228, Columbia(Am)PG32121 |
| B22923-1 | IF I WERE YOU | CBS(Eu)68230, Columbia(Am)PG32127 |

BILLIE HOLIDAY AND HER ORCHESTRA:

Bernard Anderson (tp); Buster Bailey (cl); Babe Russin (ts); Claude Thornhill (p); Allen Reuss (g); John Kirby (b); Cozy Cole (d). *NYC. June 23, 1938*

| B23154-1 | I'M GONNA LOCK MY HEART AND THROW AWAY THE KEY | CBS(Eu)68230 Columbia(Am)PG32127 |

BILLIE HOLIDAY AND HER ORCHESTRA:

Buck Clayton (tp); Lester Young (cl,ts); Queenie Johnson (p); Freddie Green (g); Walter Page (b); Jo Jones (d). *NYC. September 15, 1938.*

B23467-1	THE VERY THOUGHT OF YOU	CBS(Eu)68228, Columbia(Am)PG32121
B23469-2	I'VE GOT A DATE WITH A DREAM – 1	CBS(Eu)68230, Columbia (Am)PG32127
B23470-2	YOU CAN'T BE MINE AND SOMEBODY ELSE'S TOO	CBS(Eu)68230, Columbia(Am)PG32127

– 1 Add Dicky Wells (tb).

TEDDY WILSON AND HIS ORCHESTRA:

Harry James (tp); Benny Morton (tb); Benny Carter, Edgar Sampson (as); Herschel Evans, Lester Young (ts); Teddy Wilson (p); Al Casey (g); Walter Page (b); Jo Jones (d). *NYC. November 9, 1938*

B23687-1	SAY IT WITH A KISS	CBS(Eu)68230,
		Columbia(Am)PG32127
B23690-2	THEY SAY	CBS(Eu)68230,
		Columbia(Am)PG32127

BILLIE HOLIDAY AND HER ORCHESTRA:

Charlie Shavers (tp); Tyree Glenn (tb); Chu Berry (ts); Sonny White (p); Al Casey (g); John Williams (b); Cozy Cole (d). *NYC. January 20, 1939*

B23992-1	THAT'S ALL I ASK OF YOU	CBS(Eu)68228,
		Columbia(Am)PG32121
B23993-1	DREAM OF LIFE	CBS(Eu)68228,
		Columbia(Am)PG32121

TEDDY WILSON AND HIS ORCHESTRA:

Roy Eldridge (tp); Benny Carter (as); Ernie Powell (cl,ts); Teddy Wilson (p); Danny Barker (g); Milt Hinton (b); Cozy Cole (d). *NYC. January 30, 1939*

B24046-2	MORE THAN YOU KNOW	CBS(Eu)68230,
		Columbia(Am)PG32127
B24047-A	SUGAR	CBS(Eu)68230,
		Columbia(Am)PG32127

BILLIE HOLIDAY AND HER ORCHESTRA:

Hot Lips Page (tp); Tab Smith (as,sop); Kenneth Hollon, Stanley Payne (ts); Ken Kersey (p); Jimmy McLin (g); John Williams (b); Eddie Dougherty (d) *NYC. March 21, 1939*

W24248-1	WHY DID I ALWAYS DEPEND	CBS(Eu)68230,
	ON YOU	Columbia(Am)PG32127
W24249-1	LONG GONE BLUES	CBS(Eu)68228,
		Columbia(Am)PG32121

With FRANKIE NEWTON AND HIS ORCHESTRA:

Frankie Newton (tp); Tab Smith (as,sop); Kenneth Hollon, Stanley Payne (ts);

Sonny White (p); Jimmy McLin (g); John Williams (b); Eddie Dougherty (d).
NYC. April 20, 1939

WP24403-A	STRANGE FRUIT	Commodore(Eu)6.24055
WP24403-B	STRANGE FRUIT	Commodore(Eu)6.24055
WP24404-A	YESTERDAYS	Commodore(Eu)6.24055
WP24404-B	YESTERDAYS	Commodore(Eu)6.24055
WP24405-A	FINE AND MELLOW	Commodore(Eu)6.24055
WP24406-A	I GOTTA RIGHT TO SING THE BLUES	Commodore(Eu)6.24055
WP24406-B	I GOTTA RIGHT TO SING THE BLUES	Commodore(Eu)6.24055

BILLIE HOLIDAY AND HER ORCHESTRA:
Charlie Shavers (tp); Tab Smith (as,sop); Kenneth Hollon, Stanley Payne (ts);
Ken Kersey (p); Jimmy McLin (g); John Williams (b); Eddie Dougherty (d).
NYC. July 5, 1939

W24877-A	SOME OTHER SPRING	CBS(Eu)68229, Columbia(Am)PG32124
W24879-A	THEM THERE EYES	CBS(Eu)68228, Columbia(Am)PG32121

BILLIE HOLIDAY AND HER ORCHESTRA:
Buck Clayton, Harry Edison (tp); Earl Warren (as); Lester Young (ts); Jack
Washington (bars,as); Joe Sullivan (p); Freddie Green (g); Walter Page (b); Jo
Jones (d). *NYC. December 13, 1939*

W23641-A	NIGHT AND DAY	CBS(Eu)68230, Columbia(Am)PG32127
W23642-A	THE MAN I LOVE	CBS(Eu)68229, Columbia(Am)PG32124
W23644-A	YOU'RE A LUCKY GUY	CBS(Eu)68230, Columbia(Am)PG32127

BILLIE HOLIDAY AND HER ORCHESTRA:
Roy Eldridge (tp); Jimmy Powell, Carl Frye (as); Kermit Scott (ts); Sonny
White (p); Lawrence Lucie (g); John Williams (b); 'Doc' West (d). *NYC.
February 29, 1940.*

W26572-A	GHOST OF YESTERDAY	CBS(Eu)68229, Columbia(Am)PG32124

W26573-A	BODY AND SOUL	CBS(Eu)68229,
		Columbia(Am)PG32124
W26575-B	FALLING IN LOVE AGAIN	CBS(Eu)68230,
		Columbia(Am)PG32127

BILLIE HOLIDAY AND HER ORCHESTRA:
Roy Eldridge (tp); Bill Bowen, Joe Eldridge (as); Lester Young, Kermit Scott (ts); Teddy Wilson (p); Freddy Green (g); Walter Page (b); J.C. Heard (d). *NYC. June 7, 1940*

W26900-A	I'M PULLING THROUGH	CBS(Eu)68229,
		Columbia(Am)PG32124
W26901-A	TELL ME MORE	CBS(Eu)68229,
		Columbia(Am)PG32124
W26902-A	LAUGHING AT LIFE	CBS(Eu)68229,
		Columbia(Am)PG32124
W26903-A	TIME ON MY HANDS	CBS(Eu)68229,
		PG32124

BILLIE HOLIDAY AND HER ORCHESTRA:
Roy Eldridge (tp); George Auld, Don Redman (as); Don Byas, Jimmy Hamilton (ts); Teddy Wilson (p); John Collins (g); Al Hall (b); Kenny Clarke (d). *NYC. September 12, 1940.*

W28617-1	I'M ALL FOR YOU	CBS(Eu)68230,
		Columbia(Am)PG32127
W28618-1	I HEAR MUSIC	CBS(Eu)68230,
		Columbia(Am)PG32127
W28619-1	IT'S THE SAME OLD STORY	CBS(Eu)68230,
		Columbia(Am)PG32127
W28620-1	PRACTISE MAKES PERFECT	CBS(Eu)68230,
		Columbia(Am)PG32127

BENNY CARTER AND HIS ALL STAR ORCHESTRA:
Bill Coleman (tp); Benny Morton (tb); Benny Carter (cl,as); George Auld (ts); Sonny White (p); Ulysses Livingston (g); Wilson Myers (b); Yank Porter (d). *NYC. October 15, 1940.*

| W28874-1 | ST. LOUIS BLUES | CBS(Eu)68230, |
| | | Columbia(Am)PG32127 |

BILLIE HOLIDAY AND HER ORCHESTRA:

Shad Collins (tp); Eddie Barefield, Leslie Johnakins (as); Lester Young (ts);
Eddie Heywood (p); John Collins (g); Ted Sturgis (b); Kenny Clarke (d). *NYC.*
March 21, 1941

W29987-1	LET'S DO IT	CBS(Eu)68230, Columbia(Am)PG32127
W29988-1	GEORGIA ON MY MIND	CBS(Eu)68229, Columbia(Am)PG32124
W29989-1	ROMANCE IN THE DARK	CBS(Eu)68229, Columbia(Am)PG32124
W29990-1	ALL OF ME	CBS(Eu)68229, Columbia(Am)PG32124

BILLIE HOLIDAY AND HER ORCHESTRA:

Roy Eldridge (tp); Jimmy Powell, Lester Boone (as); Ernie Powell (ts); Eddie
Heywood (p); Paul Chapman (g); Grachan Moncur (b); Herbie Cowans (d).
NYC. May 9, 1941

W30457-1	I'M IN A LOWDOWN GROOVE	CBS(Eu)68230, Columbia(Am)PG32127
W30458-1	GOD BLESS THE CHILD	CBS(Eu)68229, Columbia(Am)PG32124
W30459-1	AM I BLUE?	CBS(Eu)68229, Columbia(Am)PG32124
W30460-1	SOLITUDE	CBS(Eu)68230, Columbia(Am)PG32127

with TEDDY WILSON AND HIS ORCHESTRA:

Emmett Berry (tp); Hymie Schertzer (as); Jimmy Hamilton (cl,ts); Babe Russin
(ts); Teddy Wilson (p); Al Casey (g); John Williams (b); J.C. Heard (d). *NYC.*
August 7, 1941.

W31003-1	I COVER THE WATERFRONT	CBS(Eu)68229, Columbia(Am)PG32124
W31004-1	LOVE ME OR LEAVE ME	CBS(Eu)68229, Columbia(Am)PG32124
W31005-1	GLOOMY SUNDAY	CBS(Eu)68229, Columbia(Am)PG32124

With **TEDDY WILSON AND HIS ORCHESTRA**

Emmett Berry (tp); Hymie Schertzer (as); Jimmy Hamilton (cl,ts); Babe Russin (ts); Teddy Wilson (p); Gene Fields (g); John Williams (b); J.C. Heard (d). *NYC. February 10, 1942*

W32406-1	MANDY IS TWO	CBS(Eu)68230, Columbia(Am)PG32127
W32407-1	IT'S A SIN TO TELL A LIE	CBS(Eu)68230, Columbia(Am)PG32127

With **EDDIE HEYWOOD AND HIS ORCHESTRA:**

'Doc' Cheatham (tp); Vic Dickenson (tb); Lem Davis (as); Eddie Heywood (p); Teddy Walters (g); John Simmonds (b); Sid Catlett (d). *NYC. March 25, 1944*

A4742-2	HOW AM I TO KNOW	Commodore(Eu)624055
A4742-3	HOW AM I TO KNOW	Commodore(Eu)624055
A4743-1	MY OLD FLAME	Commodore(Eu)624055
A4743-2	MY OLD FLAME	Commodore(Eu)624055
A4744-1	I'LL GET BY	Commodore(Eu)624055
A4744-2	I'LL GET BY	Commodore(Eu)624055
A4745-1	I COVER THE WATERFRONT	Commodore(Eu)624055
A4745-2	I COVER THE WATERFRONT	Commodore(Eu)624055

With **EDDIE HEYWOOD AND HIS ORCHESTRA:**

'Doc' Cheatham (tp); Vic Dickenson (tb); Lem Davis (as); Eddie Heywood (p); John Simmonds (b); Sid Catlett (d). *NYC. April 1, 1944*

A4750-1	I'LL BE SEEING YOU	Commodore(Eu)6.24291
A4750-2/3	I'LL BE SEEING YOU	Commodore(Eu)6.24291
A4751-1	I'M YOURS	Commodore(Eu)6.24291
A4751-2	I'M YOURS	Commodore(Eu)6.24291
A4752-1	EMBRACEABLE YOU	Commodore(Eu)6.24291
A4752-2	EMBRACEABLE YOU	Commodore(Eu)6.24291
A4753-1	AS TIME GOES BY	Commodore(Eu)6.24291
A4753-2	AS TIME GOES BY	Commodore(Eu)6.24291

With **EDDIE HEYWOOD AND HIS ORCHESTRA:**

Eddie Heywood (p); John Simmonds (b); Sid Catlett (d). *NYC. April 8, 1944*

A4754-2	HE'S FUNNY THAT WAY	Commodore(Eu)6.24291
A4754-3	HE'S FUNNY THAT WAY	Commodore(Eu)6.24291
A4755-2	LOVER COME BACK TO ME	Commodore(Eu)6.24291
A4755-3	LOVER COME BACK TO ME	Commodore(Eu)6.24291
A4756-1	I LOVE MY MAN (Billie's blues)	Commodore(Eu)6.24291
A4756-2	I LOVE MY MAN (Billie's blues)	Commodore(Eu)6.24291
A4757-1	ON THE SUNNY SIDE OF THE STREET	Commodore(Eu)6.24291

With **TOOTS CAMERATA AND HIS ORCHESTRA**:

Russ Case (tp); Hymie Schertzer, Jack Cressy (as); Larry Binyon, Paul Ricci (ts); Dave Bowman (p); Carl Kress (g); Haig Stephens (b); Johnny Blowers (d); Six Strings; Camerata (arr). *NYC. October 4, 1944*

W72404-A	LOVER MAN	MCA(Eu)MCL1688
W72405-A	NO MORE	MCA(Eu)MCL1688

With **TOOTS CAMERATA AND HIS ORCHESTRA**:

Russ Case (tp); Hymie Schertzer, Jack Cressy (as); Larry Binyon, Dave Harris (ts); Dave Bowman (p); Carl Kress (g); Haig Stephens (b); George Wettling (d); Six Strings; Camerata (arr). *NYC. November 8, 1944*

W72497-A	THAT OLE DEVIL CALLED LOVE	MCA(Eu)MCL1688

With **BOB HAGGART AND HIS ORCHESTRA**:

Joe Guy (tp); Bill Stegmeyer (as); Hank Ross, Armand Camgros (ts); Stan Webb (bars); Sammy Benskin (p); Tiny Grimes (g); Bob Haggart (t); Specs Powell (d); Six strings. *NYC. August 14, 1945*

W73006-A	DON'T EXPLAIN	MCA(Eu)MCL1688
W73008-A	YOU BETTER GO NOW	MCA(Eu)MCL1688
W73009-A	WHAT IS THIS THING CALLED LOVE	MCA(Eu)MCL1688

With **BILL STEGMEYER AND HIS ORCHESTRA**:

Chris Griffin, Joe Guy (tp); Bill Stegmeyer (as); Bernard Kaufman, Armand Camgros (ts); Joe Springer (p); Tiny Grimes (g); John Simmonds (b); Sid Catlett (d); Four strings. *NYC. January 22, 1946*

| W73300-A | GOOD MORNING HEARTACHE | MCA(Eu)MCL1688 |
| W73301-A | NO GOOD MAN | MCA(Eu)MCL1688 |

BILLIE HOLIDAY AND HER ORCHESTRA:
Joe Guy (tp); Joe Springer (p); Tiny Grimes (g); Billy Taylor (b); Kelly Martin (d). *NYC. March 13, 1946*

| W73440-A | BIG STUFF | MCA(Eu)MCL1688 |

With BILLY KYLE BAND:
Joe Guy (tp); Billy Kyle (p); Jimmy Shirley (g); Thomas Barney (b); Kenny Clarke (d). *NYC. April 9, 1946*

| W73497-A | BABY, I DON'T CRY OVER YOU | MCA(Eu)MCL1688 |
| W73498-A | I'LL LOOK AROUND | MCA(Eu)MCL1688 |

With JOHN SIMMONDS AND HIS ORCHESTRA:
Rostelle Reese (tp); Lem Davis (as); Bob Dorsey (ts); Bobby Tucker (p); John Simmonds (b); Denzil Best (d). *NYC. December 27, 1946*

| W73767-A | THE BLUES ARE BREWIN' | MCA(Eu)MCL1688 |
| W73768-A | GUILTY | MCA(Eu)MCL1688 |

With BOB HAGGART AND HIS ORCHESTRA:
Billy Butterfield (tp); Bill Stegmeyer (cl,as); Toots Mondello (as); Al Klink, Hank Ross (ts); Art Drellinger (bars); Bobby Tucker (p); Danny Perry (g); Bob Haggart (b); Bunny Shawker (d). *NYC. February 13, 1947*

W73792-A	DEEP SONG	MCA(Eu)MCL1688
W73793-A	THERE IS NO GREATER LOVE	MCA(Eu)MCL1688
W73794-A	EASY LIVING	MCA(Eu)MCL1688
W73795-A	SOLITUDE	MCA(Eu)MCL1776

With BOBBY TUCKER TRIO:
Bobby Tucker (p); Mundell Lowe (g); John Levey (b); Denzil Best (d); and The Stardusters (vocals). *NYC. December 10, 1948*

| W74650-A | WEEP NO MORE | MCA(Eu)MCL1776 |

W74651-A	GIRLS WERE MADE TO TAKE CARE OF BOYS	MCA(Eu)MCL1776
W74652-A	PORGY	MCA(Eu)MCL1776
W74653-A	MY MAN	MCA(Eu)MCL1776

With BUSTER HARDING AND HIS ORCHESTRA:
Emmett Berry, Jimmy Nottingham, Buck Clayton (tp); Dickie Wells, George Matthews (tb); Rudy Powell, George Dorsey (as); Lester Young, Joe Thomas (ts); Sol Moore (bars); Horace Henderson (p); Mundell Lowe (g); George Duvivier (b); Shadow Wilson (d). *NYC. August 17, 1949*

| W75147-A | T'AIN'T NOBODY'S BUSINESS IF I DO | MCA(Eu)MCL1776 |
| W75148-A | BABY GET LOST | MCA(Eu)MCL1776 |

With SY OLIVER AND HIS ORCHESTRA:
Bernie Privin, Dick Vance, Tony Faso (tp); Henderson Chambers, Morty Bullman (tb); Johnny Mince, George Dorsey (as); Budd Johnson, Fred Williams (ts); Eddie Barefield (bars,cl); Horace Henderson (p); Everett Barksdale (g); George Duvivier (b); Cozy Cole (d). *NYC. August 29, 1949*

| W75203-A | KEEPS ON RAININ' | MCA(Eu)MCL1776 |
| W75204-A | THEM THERE EYES | MCA(Eu)MCL1776 |

With SY OLIVER AND HIS ORCHESTRA:
Buck Clayton, Shad Collins, Bob Williams (tp); Henderson Chambers, George Stevenson (tb); Pete Clark, George Dorsey (as); Budd Johnson, Fred Williams (ts); Dave McRae (bars); Horace Henderson (p); Everett Barksdale (g); Joe Benjamin (b); Wallace Bishop (d). *NYC. September 8, 1949*

| W75241-A | DO YOUR DUTY | MCA(Eu)MCL1776 |
| W75242-A | GIMME A PIGFOOT AND A BOTTLE OF BEER | MCA(Eu)MCL1776 |

With LOUIS ARMSTRONG and SY OLIVER AND HIS ORCHESTRA:
Bernie Privin (tp); Johnny Mince, Sid Cooper (as); Art Drellinger, Pat Nizza (ts); Billy Kyle (p); Everett Barksdale (g); Joe Benjamin (b); James Crawford (d); Louis Armstrong (tp,vcl). *NYC. September 30, 1949*

| W75342-A | YOU CAN'T LOSE A A BROKEN HEART | MCA(Eu)MCL1772 |

| W75343-A | MY SWEET HUNK O'TRASH | MCA(Eu)MCL1772 |
| W75344-A | NOW OR NEVER – 1 | MCA(Eu)MCL1776 |

– 1 omit Louis Armstrong. Other titles on MCL1772 do not feature
Billie Holiday.

With GORDON JENKINS AND HIS ORCHESTRA:

Bobby Hackett (tp); Milt Yayner (as,cl); John Fulton (ts,cl,fl); Bernie Leighton
(p); Tony Mottola (g); Jack Lesberg (b); Bunny Shawker (d); five strings. *NYC.
October 19, 1949*

W75421-A	YOU'RE MY THRILL	MCA(Eu)MCL1776
W75422-A	CRAZY HE CALLS ME	MCA(Eu)MCL1776
W75423-A	PLEASE TELL ME NOW	MCA(Eu)MCL1776
W75424-A	SOMEBODY'S ON MY MIND	MCA(Eu)MCL1776

with Dent Eckles (fl,saxs); Charlie LaVere (p); Bob Bain (g); Lou Butterman
(b); Nick Fatool (d); four strings; choir. *LA. March 8, 1950*

| L5416 | GOD BLESS THE CHILD | MCA(Eu)MCL1776 |
| L5417 | THIS IS HEAVEN TO ME | MCA(Eu)MCL1776 |

BILLIE HOLIDAY AND HER ORCHESTRA

Charlie Shavers (tp); Flip Phillips (ts); Oscar Peterson (p); Barney Kessel (g);
Ray Brown (b); Alvin Stoller (d). *LA. March 26, 1952*

764-3	EAST OF THE SUN	Verve(Eu)2610027
765-1	BLUE MOON	Verve(Eu)2610027
766-1	YOU GO TO MY HEAD	Verve(Eu)2610027
767-2	YOU TURNED THE TABLES ON ME	Verve(Eu)2610027
768-1	EASY TO LOVE	Verve(Eu)2610027
769-3	THESE FOOLISH THINGS	Verve(Eu)2610027
770-3	I ONLY HAVE EYES FOR YOU	Verve(Eu)2610027
771-1	SOLITUDE	Verve(Eu)2610027

BILLIE HOLIDAY AND HER ORCHESTRA:

Charlie Shavers (tp); Flip Phillips (ts); Oscar Peterson (p); Barney Kessel (g);
Ray Brown (b); J.C. Heard (d). *LA. April 1952*

784-1	EVERYTHING I HAVE IS YOURS	Verve(Eu)2610027
785-4	LOVE FOR SALE	Verve(Eu)2610027
786-4	MOONGLOW	Verve(Eu)2610027
787-3	TENDERLY	Verve(Eu)2610027
788-2	IF THE MOON TURNS GREEN	Verve(Eu)2610027
789-3	REMEMBER	Verve(Eu)2610027
790-7	AUTUMN IN NEW YORK	Verve(Eu)2610027

BILLIE HOLIDAY AND HER ORCHESTRA:
Joe Newman (tp); Paul Quinichette (ts); Oscar Peterson (p,organ); Freddie Green (g); Ray Brown (b); Gus Johnson (d). *NYC. July 27, 1952*

839-6	MY MAN	Verve(Eu)2610027
840-4	LOVER COME BACK TO ME	Verve(Eu)2610027
841-3	STORMY WEATHER	Verve(Eu)2610027
842-2	YESTERDAYS	Verve(Eu)2610027
843-2	HE'S FUNNY THAT WAY	Verve(Eu)2610027
844-3	I CAN'T FACE THE MUSIC	Verve(Eu)2610027

BILLIE HOLIDAY AND HER ORCHESTRA:
Charlie Shavers (tp); Oscar Peterson (p); Herb Ellis (g); Ray Brown (b); Ed Shaughnessy (d) *NYC. April 14, 1954*

1566-1	I CRIED FOR YOU	Verve(Eu)2610027
1567-1	HOW DEEP IS THE OCEAN	Verve(Eu)2610027
1568-1	WHAT A LITTLE MOONLIGHT CAN DO	Verve(Eu)2610027

BILLIE HOLIDAY AND HER ORCHESTRA:
Harry Edison (tp); Willie Smith (as); Bobby Tucker (p); Barney Kessel (g); Red Callender (b); Chico Hamilton (d). *LA. September 3, 1954*

1932-6	TOO MARVELLOUS FOR WORDS	Verve(Eu)2610038
1933	P.S. I LOVE YOU	Verve(Eu)2610038
1934	SOFTLY	Verve(Eu)2610038
1935-3	I THOUGHT ABOUT YOU	Verve(Eu)2610038

1936-2	LOVE ME OR LEAVE ME	Verve(Eu)2610038
1937-1	WILLOW WEEP FOR ME	Verve(Eu)2610038
1938-3	STORMY BLUES	Verve(Eu)2610038

BILLIE HOLIDAY AND HER ORCHESTRA:
Charlie Shavers (tp); Tony Scott (cl); Budd Johnson (ts); Carl Drinkard (p); Billy Bauer (g); Leonard Gaskin (b); Cozy Cole (d). *NYC. February 14, 1955*

2274-4	SAY IT ISN'T SO	Verve(Eu)2610038
2275-5	I'VE GOT MY LOVE TO KEEP ME WARM	Verve(Eu)2610038
2276-4	I WISHED ON THE MOON	Verve(Eu)2610038
2277-3	ALWAYS	Verve(Eu)2610038
2278-2	EVERYTHING HAPPENS TO ME	Verve(Eu)2610038
2279-2	DO NOTHING 'TIL YOU HEAR FROM ME	Verve(Eu)2610038
2280-2	AIN'T MISBEHAVIN'	Verve(Eu)2610038

BILLIE HOLIDAY AND HER ORCHESTRA:
Harry Edison (tp); Benny Carter (as); Jimmy Rowles (p); Barney Kessel (g); John Simmons (b); Larry Bunker (d). *LA. August 23, 1955*

2438-2	I DON'T WANT TO CRY ANYMORE	Verve(Eu)2610038
2439-3	PRELUDE TO A KISS	Verve(Eu)2610038
2440-1	GHOST OF A CHANCE	Verve(Eu)2610038
2441-3	WHEN YOUR LOVER HAS GONE	Verve(Eu)2610038
2442-4	GONE WITH THE WIND	Verve(Eu)2610038
2443-2	PLEASE DON'T TALK ABOUT ME WHEN I'M GONE	Verve(Eu)2610038
2444-1	IT HAD TO BE YOU	Verve(Eu)2610038
2445-5	NICE WORK IF YOU CAN GET IT	Verve(Eu)2610038

BILLIE HOLIDAY AND HER ORCHESTRA:
Harry Edison (tp); Benny Carter (as); Jimmy Rowles (p); Barney Kessel (g); John Simmons (b); Larry Bunker (d). *LA. August 25, 1955*

| 2446-3 | COME RAIN OR COME SHINE | Verve(Eu)2610038 |

2447-1	I'VE GOT A RIGHT TO SING THE BLUES	Verve(Eu)2610038
2448-3	WHAT'S NEW	Verve(Eu)2610053
2449-8	A FINE ROMANCE	Verve(Eu)2610053
2450-1	I HADN'T ANYONE 'TIL YOU	Verve(Eu)2610053
2451-3	I GET A KICK OUT OF YOU	Verve(Eu)2610053
2452-2	EVERYTHING I HAVE IS YOURS	Verve(Eu)2610053
2453-3	ISN'T THIS A LOVELY DAY	Verve(Eu)2610053

With TONY SCOTT AND HIS ORCHESTRA:

Charlie Shavers (tp); Tony Scott (cl,arr); Paul Quinichette (ts); Wynton Kelly (p); Kenny Burrell (g); Aaron Bell (b); Lennie McBrowne (d). *NYC. June 7, 1956*

2850-5	TRAV'LIN' LIGHT	Verve(Eu)2610053
2851-3	I MUST HAVE THAT MAN	Verve(Eu)2610053
2853-1	SOME OTHER SPRING	Verve(Eu)2610053
2854-4	LADY SINGS THE BLUES	Verve(Eu)2610053
2855-12	STRANGE FRUIT	Verve(Eu)2610053
2856-1	GOD BLESS THE CHILD	Verve(Eu)2610053
2857-8	GOOD MORNING HEARTACHE	Verve(Eu)2610053
2858-1	NO GOOD MAN	Verve(Eu)2610053

BILLIE HOLIDAY AND HER ORCHESTRA:

Harry Edison (tp); Ben Webster (ts); Jimmy Rowles (p); Barney Kessel (g); Joe Mondragon (b); Alvin Stoller (d). *LA. August 14, 1956.*

2914-3	DO NOTHIN' TILL YOU HEAR FROM ME	Verve(Eu)2610053
2915-6	CHEEK TO CHEEK	Verve(Eu)2610053
2916-4	ILL WIND	Verve(Eu)2610053
2917-8	SPEAK LOW	Verve(Eu)2610053

BILLIE HOLIDAY AND HER ORCHESTRA:

Harry Edison (tp); Ben Webster (ts); Jimmy Rowles (p); Barney Kessel (g); Joe Mondragon (g); Alvin Stoller (d). *LA. August 18, 1956*

| 2929-4 | WE'LL BE TOGETHER AGAIN | Verve(Eu)2610053 |

2930-3	ALL OR NOTHING AT ALL	Verve(Eu)2610053
2931-6	SOPHISTICATED LADY	Verve(Eu)2610053
2932-6	APRIL IN PARIS	Verve(Eu)2610053

BILLIE HOLIDAY AND HER ORCHESTRA:
Harry Edison (tp); Ben Webster (ts); Jimmy Rowles (p); Barney Kessel (g); Red
Mitchell (b); Alvin Stoller (d). *LA. January 3, 1957*

| 20499-1 | MOONLIGHT IN VERMONT | Verve(Eu)2304340 |
| 20500-6 | A FOGGY DAY | Verve(Eu)2304243 |

BILLIE HOLIDAY AND HER ORCHESTRA:
Harry Edison (tp); Ben Webster (ts); Jimmy Rowles (p); Barney Kessel (g); Red
Mitchell (b); Alvin Stoller (d). *LA. January 4, 1957*

20501-2	I DIDN'T KNOW WHAT TIME IT WAS	Verve(Eu)2304243
20502-8	JUST ONE OF THOSE THINGS	Verve(Eu)2304243
20503-4	COMES LOVE	Verve(Eu)2304340

BILLIE HOLIDAY AND HER ORCHESTRA:
Harry Edison (tp); Ben Webster (ts); Jimmy Rowles (p); Barney Kessel (g); Red
Mitchell (b); Alvin Stoller (d). *LA. January 7, 1957*

20504-1	DAY IN DAY OUT	Verve(Eu)2304243
20505-3	DARN THAT DREAM	Verve(Eu)2304340
20507-1	BODY AND SOUL	Verve(Eu)2304340

BILLIE HOLIDAY AND HER ORCHESTRA:
Harry Edison (tp); Ben Webster (ts); Jimmy Rowles (p); Barney Kessel (g); Red
Mitchell (b); Alvin Stoller (d). *LA. January 8, 1957*

| 20561-1 | STARS FELL ON ALABAMA | Verve(Eu)2304243 |
| 20564-3 | ONE FOR MY BABY | Verve(Eu)2304243 |

BILLIE HOLIDAY AND HER ORCHESTRA:

Harry Edison (tp); Ben Webster (ts); Jimmy Rowles (p); Barney Kessel (g); Red Mitchell (b); Larry Bunker (d). *LA. January 9, 1957*

20565-3	THEY CAN'T TAKE THAT AWAY FROM ME	Verve(Eu)2304340
20566-1	EMBRACEABLE YOU	Verve(Eu)2304340
20567-4	LETS CALL THE WHOLE THING OFF	Verve(Eu)2304340
20568-6	GEE BABY AINT I GOOD TO YOU	Verve(Eu)2304340

With RAY ELLIS AND HIS ORCHESTRA:

Large concert orchestra with brass, reeds, strings, rhythm plus vocal choir. *NYC. February 18, 1958*

C060460	YOU DON'T KNOW WHAT LOVE IS	CBS(Eu)32259, Columbia(Am)PC8048
C060461	I'LL BE AROUND	CBS(Eu)32259, Columbia(Am)PC8048
C060462	FOR HEAVEN'S SAKE	CBS(Eu)32259, Columbia(Am)PC8048
C060463	BUT BEAUTIFUL	CBS(Eu)32259, Columbia(Am)PC8048

With RAY ELLIS AND HIS ORCHESTRA:

Large concert orchestra with brass, reeds, strings, rhythm plus vocal choir. *NYC. February 19, 1958*

C060464	FOR ALL WE KNOW	CBS(Eu)32259, Columbia(Am)PC8048
C060465	IT'S EASY TO REMEMBER	CBS(Eu)32259, Columbia(Am)PC8048
C060466	I'M A FOOL TO WANT YOU	CBS(Eu)32259, Columbia(Am)PC8048

With RAY ELLIS AND HIS ORCHESTRA:
Large concert orchestra with brass, reeds, strings, rhythm plus vocal choir.
NYC. February 20, 1958

C060467	THE END OF A LOVE AFFAIR	(see note at the end of discography).
C060468	GLAD TO BE UNHAPPY	CBS(Eu)32259, Columbia(Am)PC8048
C060469	YOU'VE CHANGED	CBS(Eu)32259, Columbia(Am)PC8048
C060470	I GET ALONG WITHOUT YOU VERY WELL	CBS(Eu)32259, Columbia(Am)PC8048
C060471	VIOLETS FOR YOUR FURS	CBS(Eu)32259, Columbia(Am)PC8048

With RAY ELLIS AND HIS ORCHESTRA:
Harp; four strings; Jimmy Cleveland (tb); Romeo Penque (as,ts,bass cl); Hank Jones (p); Kenny Burrell (g); Joe Benjamin (b); Osie Johnson (d). *NYC. March 3, 1959*

59XY435	ALL THE WAY	MGM(Eu)2304392
59XY436	IT'S NOT FOR ME TO SAY	MGM(Eu)2304392
59XY437	I'LL NEVER BE THE SAME	MGM(Eu)2304392
59XY438	JUST ONE MORE CHANCE	MGM(Eu)2304392

With RAY ELLIS AND HIS ORCHESTRA:
Twelve strings; Harry Edison (tp); Jimmy Cleveland (tb); Gene Quill (as); Hank Jones (p); Barry Galbraith (g); Milt Hinton (b); Osie Johnson (d). *NYC. March 4, 1959*

59XY439	SLEEPY TIME DOWN SOUTH	MGM(Eu)2304392
59XY440	DON'T WORRY 'BOUT ME	MGM(Eu)2304392
59XY441	SOMETIMES I'M HAPPY	MGM(Eu)2304392
59XY442	YOU TOOK ADVANTAGE OF ME	MGM(Eu)2304392

With **RAY ELLIS AND HIS ORCHESTRA:**

Harry Edison, Joe Wilder (tp); Billy Byers (tb); Al Cohn (ts); Danny Bank (bars); Hank Jones (p); Barry Galbraith (g); Milt Hinton (b); Osie Johnson (d). *NYC. March 11, 1959*

59XY455	THERE'LL BE SOME CHANGES MADE	MGM(Eu)2304392
59XY456	'DEED I DO	MGM(Eu)2304392
59XY457	ALL OF YOU	MGM(Eu)2304392
59XY458	BABY, WON'T YOU PLEASE COME HOME	MGM(Eu)2304392

Note:

"The End of a Love Affair" was included on some early pressings of 'Lady in Satin' so it may be worth seeking a second hand copy containing this track.

TITLE'S OF (Eu) LP'S LISTED IN THE MAIN DISCOGRAPHY

Except where noted American equivalents have the same titles. 2LP means a double LP all others are single LP's. Country of issue follows title.

    68228 – *The Billie Holiday Story, Volume 1*, 2LP – United Kingdom
    68229 – *The Billie Holiday Story, Volume 2*, 2LP – Holland
    68230 – *The Billie Holiday Story, Volume 3*, 2LP – Holland
  6.24055 – *Fine and Mellow* – West Germany
  6.24291 – *I'll be seeing you* – West Germany
MCL1688 – *16 Classic tracks* – United Kingdom
MCL1776 – *Billie Holiday, Volume 2* – United Kingdom
MCL1772 – *Louis and friends* – United Kingdom
 2610027 – *The First Verve Sessions* – 2LP – France
 2610038 – *Stormy blues* – 2LP – France
 2610053 – *All or nothing at all* – 2LP – France
 2304243 – *Song for distingués lovers* – France
 2304340 – *Body and soul* – France
   32259 – *Lady in Satin* – United Kingdom
 2304392 – *Last recording* – France

Further listening suggestions:
Verve 2317059 – *Lady sings the blues* – 14 tracks selected from,
    Verve recordings 1946-1958. United Kingdom.
Audiofidelity AFEB1050 – *Don't Explain* – 3LP set of concert, club, radio and
    T.V. shows including some titles from the main discography. Dates from
    1937 to 1958. United Kingdom.
Verve UMV2520 – *Billie Holiday at Jazz at the Philharmonic* – 1946 concert
    recording including an emotional version of 'Strange Fruit'. Currently only
    available as a Japanese import.
CBS66267 – *God bless the child* – 2LP set containing alternate verions of CBS/
    Columbia recordings featured in 'The Billie Holiday Story'.
    United Kingdom. CB30782(Am)
Verve 2304343 – *Carnegie Hall 1956 concert* – Billie Holiday sings songs
    reflecting her life, interspersed with narrations by Gilbert Millstein from the
    then recently published autobiography 'Lady sings the blues'. – France.
Columbia CL637 – *Ladyday* – Highly recommended issue, none of the tracks
    duplicate Columbia/CBS titles in the main discography.(Am).
Capitol 2 C068-86527 – *Billie Holiday 1942-1951- 1954* – Neatly gathers
    together the only known title recorded for Capitol in 1942 'Travelling light';
    four tracks recorded for Aladdin in 1951 plus a 1954 concert performance
    in Germany. France.
Reading suggestions: "Born to sing the blues" – A discography of Billie
    Holiday – by Jack Millar – published in Copenhagen. "Billie's blues" by
    John Chilton – published in Great Britian.

After the Albert Hall concert, London, February 1954